"Man will find the greatest riches where he finds the joy in living."

****

"The only thing that is certain for man is change. To battle change is to waste one's time...to become the willing ally of change is to assure oneself of life."

****

"Don't spend your precious time asking 'Why isn't the world a better place?' It will only be time wasted. The question to ask is 'How can I make it better?' To that question, there is an answer."

****

"The new and the old have value to man only as they relate to the present...To live for either is to lose his only reality, the moment."

****

"Pride and impatience in man may not be virtues, but sometimes there is a certain beauty in both."

****

"Man must learn to let go as easily as he grasps or he will find his hands full and his mind empty."

****

"Though every hello is the beginning of a goodbye, do not lose heart; for every goodbye may also be the beginning of another hello."

by Leo Buscaglia, Ph.D.

FREDDY THE LEAF

BECAUSE I AM HUMAN

THE DISABLED AND THEIR PARENTS:
  A Counseling Challenge

THE WAY OF THE BULL

Published by Fawcett Crest and Columbine Books:

LOVE

LIVING, LOVING & LEARNING

PERSONHOOD

LEO BUSCAGLIA, Ph.D.

The Way of the Bull

FAWCETT CREST • NEW YORK

A Fawcett Crest Book
Published by Ballantine Books

Library of Congress Catalog Card Number: 73-83777

ISBN 0-449-20090-6

This edition published by arrangement with Charles B. Slack,
Inc.

Manufactured in the United States of America

First Ballantine Books Edition: March 1983
Tenth printing: April 1984

Interior illustrations by Roberta Ludlow

This book is dedicated to . . .

Those with no concern for the Way;
Those temporarily lost on the Way;
Those diligently seeking the Way;
Those who know, but are unable to follow the Way;
Those who simply live the Way;

For all of us are one.

Table
of
Contents

Introduction

The title, THE WAY OF THE BULL, was suggested by a Zen book, *10 Bulls,* written in the 12th century by the Chinese Zen master, Kakuan. In his story the bull represented life energy, truth and action. The way concerned the steps that man might take in the process of seeking insight, finding himself, discovering his true nature.

During the years of my life I have been schooled by our society in many things. Mostly, I learned and never questioned. Surely my teachers, who purported to love me, would not lead me down false paths into dead ends, away from myself into loneliness and despair.

A few years ago, I became suspicious. I began to believe in my own senses, to trust my own mind. It soon became painfully obvious that much of what I had been taught had served as the greatest deterrent to joy and finding myself and had led me rather into my greatest fears, disappointments, confusions and pain.

For example, my society had taught me that man's worth was to be measured by the things he possessed. If he owned a "big" car, a "lavish" home and an "impressive" bank balance, he must be an important and worthy man, and was to be emulated. I was never told that man "possesses" nothing, only himself. I began to wonder: If man is his "things," what happens to him when he loses them or they are taken away from him?

I was also taught that life had no meaning unless it was goal-oriented and that my life, to be meaningful, had to be spent in creating goals, making decisions about those goals and charging toward them, through mud and muck if necessary, to achieve them.

Time and experience revealed to me that life was a trip, not a goal. That often one became so fixed on the end that he totally missed life along the way, and found, only too late, that when he had scaled the mountain there was only another mountain, and another, and another. What a pity that he had never stopped long enough to breathe the new, clean, fresh air and admire the spectacular view. I had to question: If life is a continual trip, does it matter if one ever "gets" anywhere?

Society also created confusing dichotomies for me: good and bad, mature and immature, reality and fantasy. I was then forced to select, supposedly for my own well-being, one over the other. I was told that society's morality was always superior to my own, though my true nature was compelled to question this. I asked, for example: Does it make sense that wars are fought to preserve peace?

The idea that maturity came with age, that experience meant wisdom, that youth could never be wiser than their elders, conflicted with my experience, which saw no real correlation. Had the wise elders really made our world a better place for us to live in?

The constant advice that I "get out of my fantasy world" into "reality," that I "face reality" often proved frustrating, since society's reality constantly seemed more unreal than my fantasy. I pondered: Wasn't reality nothing more than the freezing, the firming up, of illusion?

But so successfully had I learned these lessons, heard and responded to these teachings that it was only a little more than ten years ago that I decided to listen to myself, follow my own voices, and go the WAY that seemed to be most congruent with me and my true nature. In other words, I decided to take THE WAY OF THE BULL.

This WAY has not always been easy, though it has been wondrous, full of excitement and discovery, even though I now know that one need never "go" anywhere to find himself, for he is already "there."

Along my WAY I have read many books, experienced a million amazing things and met wondrous people in strange lands. Each has served to open my mind and head and heart. From each I have learned much. I know, now, for instance, that my existence is to be found nowhere but in myself for my existence *is* me. I know that I need not hold onto experience to make it mine, the experience is enough.

I have learned, most importantly, that a WAY will only have reality as it relates to living in the now for, as stated above, life isn't the goal, it's the voyage, and the only reality seems to lie in change. But if all things that are, are already ours, then even change is an illusion, and the WAY becomes simply an unfolding, like the opening of a flower, for all things necessary are already a part of us and to discover it we need but nurture the flower, be patient and continue to grow.

LEO BUSCAGLIA
Los Angeles, 1973

chapter 1

Japan

The new and the old have value to us only as they relate to the present. Yesterday made us what we are today, tomorrow is our dream. To live for either is to lose our only reality, the moment.

The Itos

There are several Buddhist monasteries in Kamakura, the city of the Giant Daibatsu. Here among the giant bamboo and tall pine, students of Buddhism wander, ponder and perform the many functions which aid in the complex process of "seeing into the self." In this city there are numerous fantastic temples with carved ceilings, straight, clean architecture and clear-lacquered woods in beautiful natural settings.

The sea rumbles just a few steps from the city's center, and the wind rustles the trees pushing them into odd, distorted patterns like oversized bonsai. From time to time the train from Tokyo passes noisily on its way to Yokohama—whistling through the city, breaking the silence only long enough to drop off passengers and the continual hordes of sightseers who come and go; but most of the time the city sleeps naturally and peacefully in the lap of nature, very much at home in the small rolling hills that surround it.

I was the guest of Mr. and Mrs. Ito, a middle-aged and charming couple, who clung to the old and the quaint of Japan as naturally as the flowers that graced the garden in which their home was located.

The house was a rather large wooden structure, surrounded by a neat, trim, dwarf garden that rolled in green mossy splendor between tiny stone paths, among large rocks, around little bridges and finally down over the banks of a miniature stream. A large fish pond was active with bright, fat, golden and silver fish. The fence which enclosed the garden was of bamboo, old and brown with the color of time but still sturdy and well kept.

There were three large bedrooms, a room for cooking, with a huge hibachi that also served to heat the house, and a bathroom with a deep sunken tub of natural stone. Every wall was so made as to fold quickly to one side and at once make each room a part of the garden.

I had met Mr. Ito when I was guest lecturer at the English Speaking Society of a major university in Tokyo. In addition to serving as faculty advisor for the Society, he was a lecturer in comparative literature. He had studied in America, where he and his wife spent many happy and interesting hours learning what they called "The Way of the Westerner."

After my lecture, Mr. Ito approached me, "In the real sense, are not all schools of psychology simply a search for the self? They seem to claim that man is incapable of pursuing the 'self' alone, that he needs the aid and guidance of another."

"My interest stems from the fact that I am at present paralleling the teachings of psychology with our Zen Buddhism," he continued. "Do you know Zen?"

Our first discussion led to several meetings at tea rooms and beer halls all around Tokyo, and the final inquiry,

"Would you like to visit a Zen monastery? I can arrange it, you know. Near my home in Kamakura is one of the very finest Zen schools in the country. Onomito is one of the great teachers and he speaks English. I think it may prove very interesting to you. I believe it has something to offer your Western mind."

I told him I would be excited to have such an opportunity and within a few days all was arranged. I would live for a period with the monks in the monastery spending the remaining time in Mr. Ito's home which would be more comfortable while I continued my study.

Onomito, my teacher, was a short, quite powerful man with a shaved, well-shaped head and keen eyes. His hands were strong and his fingers smooth, long and thin. His kimono was wrapped about him with determination, his back was straight and—though it seldom happened—his lips always seemed on the verge of parting into a warm smile. His command of English was good though the pronunciation was difficult for him. He spoke slowly, choosing his words carefully.

"Since you are here so brief a time, you can only look," Onomito said. "Without help you will see only the things you are ready to see. I will try to help you perceive things as they are, but when days must be counted, perception is shadowed by time. If you came here as a novice, you would wait for several days before admission to Brotherhood would be granted. You would be asked to wait for a week or ten days outside the gate. We would discourage you from waiting. Our meditation hall is always full. Our modern youth, like yours in America, find it difficult to wait. Zen has not and has never had a popular appeal in Japan for it is difficult for most men to wait. Zen calls for discipline and requires that one have great courage and perseverance; that one be able to postpone the sought-after goal for an indefinite period of time without the security of knowing that he will ever attain it. There are no diplomas for the enlightenment achieved, no graduation exercise for those who have successfully pursued and found the self, and there is no monetary recognition. For this reason, it does not appeal to everyone. Hours, even lifetimes, are spent in meditation. The most important task in a monastery is learning the skill of zazen, meditation. This, with the proper teacher, can help the novice gain personal insight; it is only for this reason that such a monastery as this has any reason for existing."

We went through the monastery. Meditation halls, like large unfurnished classrooms, made up the greatest number of the cluster of buildings. There were simple rooms for lodging, a large bath, and a small kitchen. Comforts, or any signs of luxury, were conspicuously absent.

I was given a kesa (robe) and taken to the guest room. This room, like all the others, was but four walls and a series of tatami mats. Traveling monks were always allowed to stay here at least one night while en route. They were allowed the same privileges as the host monks, but stayed in the guest room.

The routine of the monastic life was given me. Basically, it was a life of prayer and meditation. Three meals, small and simple, were taken during the day. "The mind does not work well when the stomach is overfull. A full stomach is conducive only to sleep."

There are definite hours for meditation. The monks are required to sit in the proper formal posture, right foot over the left thigh, left foot over the right thigh. The hands, too, have a definite place, right hand on the left leg with palm up and on this the left hand is placed, with the thumbs pressed together over the palm. With head up and back erect but not rigid, eyes slightly open and tongue on the roof of the mouth with lips closed, one relaxes and breathes regularly.

Relaxation in this position sounded impossible to me and—for my tall, stiff body—was just that. Everyone else seemed to feel the prescribed position was surprisingly comfortable and extremely conducive to contemplation, for with each part of the body being strictly disciplined in its proper place, there was no need for fidgeting or readjusting. In position, I felt like a badly tied Christmas package about ready to come undone. It was necessary for me to concentrate so completely on staying in position that contemplation on anything else was obviously impossible. Least of all did I seem or feel peaceful and at ease, which, after all, was the objective. I was allowed, after a few tragically comic attempts, to assume the half-crossed leg position: left leg on the right thigh. This was less difficult. "The position is, in reality, only a tool and not a necessity," I was told.

Work is also a regular part of the daily routine. Each monk has his task. Tools are simple and no mechanization is allowed. Simple physical labor is the goal. Each monk, too, must go out for takuhatsu (alms). This serves a twofold function. Since the use of money is not allowed in a monastery, the food obtained through begging is the sole source of subsistence. Even more importantly, begging teaches that one is dependent upon the good will of others and teaches humility.

There is silent prayer and there are periods of communal prayer. All prayer concerns a plea for "Right Knowledge" and for the ability to hold firmly to a desire for truth.

The meals were simple—gruel, pickles, rice—but eaten in quiet decorum with the greatest reverence.

While in the monastery, I was allowed no more freedom or special privilege than any other monk. From the moment Mr. Hito left me on the first day, I was assured I had no more significance than the grains of sand which surrounded the large pine trees that shaded the monastery. There was a Westerner on the grounds, that was known as I was introduced to the entire assemblage, but it was also indicated that this was nothing special.

I saw Onomito, my sensei, only on a prearranged interview schedule. The rest of the time I was alone. I was to spend my first days trying to "feel" what was about me in the darkness of my room. This was to be accomplished through quiet—indifference to my own presence, strict silence and the inner and outer peace which these things would create. I was to rid myself of mind and achieve a state of no-mind. At first, the result was totally adverse. The feeling of being alone and unguided was completely devastating. I felt lost, confused and frightened. I longed for direction— a book to read, a person with whom to converse. I had no idea what to do with my new found stillness. I had no idea how to begin the process, if indeed it was, of ridding myself of my mind. I wished for a book of directions to read, a how-to for no-mind. But faced with nothing but myself and the most simple routine, I began to settle down. Although I had nothing to "do" and was not to "think" (the only ready tools I had ever used to accomplish any task), I found that there *was* another way to learn to "see."

My first trip from my room was beautiful. All at once, everything seemed to become alive, as if I were seeing it all for the first time. The tall pines took on subtle details. Rays of sunlight through their branches became spotlights for dancing dust. Bits of green moss took on delicate designs beneath small round dots of dew. Insects spread their tiny legs to the warmth of the sun. Puddles of water became bottomless seas with sunlight swimming in them. Shadows on smooth wood accentuated the wood grain until it seemed to hold great canyons of light and shadow. The curve of the bamboo leaf and the cascade of the motionless branch seemed to give sound in silence. Nothing was insignificant. It was necessary at times to close my eyes to keep from going sight-mad but there was no turning it off. It was all still there. I welcomed it. Why would I wish to turn it off?

I had my first interview with Onomito on the third day. He was pleasant, formal, much like the first time I had seen him. We talked of many things; my panic in silence, my difficulty in letting my mind go, and the deep awareness which had suddenly become mine.

"Yes, it is such a great waste. This ability to 'see' belongs to everyone," he said quietly; "it is always there but cannot come through the great haze of confusion until we do something to clear the haze."

Onomito explained the importance Zen places on the moment. "It is difficult for the Western mind to understand Zen primarily because of the difference in emphasis on the value of the moment. For Zen, nothing is of greater value than the moment. Life is now. Yesterday is past and gone and therefore unreal, only real in its effect on the moment. The future is not real, and possibly it will never be more than simply a dream. This leaves simply the now, the moment, as reality. "Yet," he said, "so many people live only under the shadow of the successes or mistakes of the past or the possibilities and hopes of the future. They do not seem to realize that when they deal with these worlds of the unreal, they are missing the 'moments,' the accumulation of which make a life. Life, then, becomes a series of moments, either lived or lost. Since moments pass, as time, there is soon nothing left and life is over, leaving some poor, unfortunate souls having never lived at all."

He then gave me a koan to ponder. These are spiritual lessons not to be answered by analytical means or scientific method or with knowledge, but by simply allowing the mind to arrive at truth intuitively and spiritually. For me, there was nothing simple about this process.

The first koan went something like this:

There was a Buddhist monk who one day found himself running from a hungry bear. The bear chased him to a cliff. There was nothing for him to do, if he did not desire to be food for the bear's hungry stomach, but jump. He did so and was able to catch hold, as he fell, of a branch of wood growing from the cliff's side. As he hung there, looking up at the hungry bear above, he heard the roar of a famished lion far below who was already waiting for him to tire, lose his grip and fall to its hungry jaws.

As the monk hung suspended, hungry bear above and starving lion below, he noticed the heads of two gophers appear from the cliff's side. At once they began gnawing on the small stump of wood to which he clung so desperately.

All at once the monk saw that just a stretch away was a small clump of wild strawberries. He calmly reached out, plucked the largest, reddest and ripest of the berries, and put it into his mouth.

"How delicious!," he said.

I had lost all awareness of time when I was told that it was time for my final interview with Onomito. Had I been there a week? A month? A year? He was more talkative than he had been during our earlier interviews. He said many things.

- I believe it is quite impossible to practice Zen, in the real sense, in your country, but there is much good in the knowledge of it.

- It will take you some time to integrate what you have learned here with your life. Your cup is full to the brim with Western ideas. Perhaps you are now more ready and less frightened to pour out a bit and make a place for new ways.

- Pattern your life after the giant bamboo. The exterior, though smooth and lovely to the touch, is tough and resistant to the sword. Within, it is soft, pliable, with much empty space for continued growth. It grows neatly and ordered, never cluttered. Alone, it rises tall and straight, always upward to the sky. There, it spreads its beauty to the sun. It leans on nothing. It makes its own way, perhaps near others, a part of others, but very much dependent upon its own strength and force. So pattern your life.

At the appointed time, Mr. Ito came for me. It was dusk. I had put on my Western clothes; they felt tight and uncomfortable.

We left the quiet monastery without farewells. Mr. Ito walked silently by my side along the small sand path which led up the hill to his home. The late afternoon was windy but the darkening sky was clear. The sea was in the air. The twisted trees waved their branches on a noisy, modern, rhythmical dance to which the shadows responded silently. We exchanged not a word.

Mrs. Ito prepared a fine dinner for me that evening. She knew what I had been eating and felt it was time for a good, substantial meal with salad, sushi, shrimp tempura, string beans and squash flower.

After dinner I felt that I should discuss my feelings with Mr. Ito but found it impossible to do so. Mr. Ito only smiled, expecting nothing. I remembered Onimoto's statement, "You don't talk Zen, you live it."

"I have questions only, no answers," I said.

"There are no answers, only questions." Mr. Ito smiled. "Words are created," he continued, "to stand for reality.

Often, after enough use, they become real for the individual, the true reality. But they are only words, so man is trapped."

My next few days were spent watching the living Zen. The Itos' entire life was a constant illustration of it: the beautiful amalgamation of the old and the new, the joy in the trip to Tokyo and the peace of afternoon walks through fields of bamboo near the sea, the calm of the tea ceremony along with quiet hours of meditation, the joy in the company of others, the peace of the garden and the single flower.

When the time came for my return to Tokyo, Mr. Ito took me to the Kamakura train station.

Somehow farewells in Japan were never the same as those in any other place in Asia. There was always, of course, the nostalgia of parting with a friend; however beyond that there was a feeling that the person was not holding onto you, that he had enjoyed you, learned from you, perhaps shared some ideas with you, and that now he was quite ready, if it was to be, to let you go on to others.

When I mentioned this to Mr. Ito, he commented that Buddha had spoken of this in his Parable of the Rhinoceros in the Khaggavisha Sutta. He quoted from the memory: "Let therefore one who dislikes separation, which must happen sooner or later from those beloved, walk alone like a rhinoceros."

What Mr. Ito did not quote from this parable was the sole section in the long sutta in which Buddha does *not* include that man should "walk alone like a rhinoceros":

> If a wise man secures a wise friend who will act in concert with him, being firmly established in good principles, he will live happily with him, overcoming all afflictions.

chapter 2

Japan

---

*The only thing that is certain for us is change.
To battle change is to waste our time; the battle
can never be won. To become the willing ally of
change is to assure ourselves of life.*

Abe-San

When I entered the modern office the group was already waiting in the conference room to greet me. There were two girls and six men, all quite young or seemingly so. It was impossible for me to guess the age of any of the Japanese. They rose and bowed as I entered. The sensei, or teacher, was a most wonderful looking man. He had a broad smile which revealed all of his treasured gold front teeth. The deep wrinkles at the edge of his eyes made him appear somewhat puckish. He asked if I would do them the honor of sitting among them and simply conversing in English so they might see how much they could participate.

I seated myself among them. "Good evening," I said to one of the boys, following my instructions. "What is your name?"

"Good evening," he answered in measured, practiced cadence after a moment's hesitation, his head down, eyes on the floor, "My name is Senure Abe."

Abe was a short, dark-haired, muscular individual. His well-shaped head and powerful shoulders were erectly supported by a strong back and chest; his cheekbones were high, his eyes thin concave slits of light, and his rather thick lips curved gracefully and serenely into a relaxed smile.

"Where do you live, Abe-san?" I asked.

"I live in Yokohama."

"Where do you work?"

"I work here in the import-export business," he answered.

"What do you for for fun?"

"For fun?" He looked at me with surprise. "For fun, I practice Judo. I go to Judo school." He smiled broadly as I passed on to the next person in line. A triumph! Not one serious mistake. He glanced toward his sensei for approval.

I moved on from one person to another. One was an artist, another a master of the tea ceremony. One said that he was courting a girl who was very difficult and he had no fun at all. Another claimed that he drank beer for fun. They responded freely, quickly catching the spirit of the conversation. There was much laughter.

The lesson was a great success. At seven o'clock, the hour for dismissal, they wanted to remain and, in turn, find out about me. The sensei suggested that we move on to a beer hall, which seemed a most proper thing to do, and that we continue our class there.

Chattering together, we walked out into the Tokyo night and headed toward the Ginza area, only a few streets away. There we entered the lobby of a large building and took an elevator to the beer hall on the roof. It was very crowded. Colored lanterns blew in the breeze amid the flash of neon. Chairs were collected from here and there and a table appeared from nowhere, carried overhead, singlehanded, with little effort by Abe-san. We arranged ourselves about it.

The sensei sat directly across the table from me, obviously very proud that his students had been so successful in their test of fire. He explained, "The students wish to have you come back to us again while you are in Tokyo. We shall be happy if you can spare the time to so honor us."

I assured them that I would be happy to continue the lessons provided that occasionally I could use our sessions as a source for the information I would need to see Tokyo and the rest of Japan properly.

Abe-san immediately offered to take me to the Judo school if I was interested. One of the young girls invited me to a tea ceremony. Another said she would be happy to escort me to a section of the city near the university, where I could find old books and prints. Others wanted me to taste the best sushi in all of Japan or to show me a lovely private garden. They were all interested in helping to satisfy my desire to see more of Japanese theater and made plans to take me to Kabuki and the Noh play.

Hours later, when we returned to the street, now more crowded than ever, everyone bowed to everyone else and went his way—except Abe-san. "Have you hunger?" he said.

"Yes," I answered, "I always have hunger."

"I know a restaurant where good noodles are made."

We started down the street together, with Abe-san pointing out the sights as we went along.

The noodles were excellent. We each had two large bowls which I learned to eat with chopsticks, to the delight of the restaurant staff who stood around and observed my every awkward movement. After we had eaten, we sat and talked. I was surprised to learn that Abe-san commuted from Yokohama daily. I had thought Yokohama was a great distance from Tokyo, but he assured me that there were express trains every few minutes from the Ginza Station which could get him home within an hour.

I expressed my amazement at Tokyo. "The city has come as rather a shock to me," I said. "I expected something different."

Abe-san laughed, "Temples? Kimonos? Tranquil tea gardens?"

"I knew Tokyo was one of the largest cities in the world, but I had hoped that some of the Japan of the Westerner's dream remained."

"Oh," he said, "there is still much to see of the Old Japan."

Abe was a university student in law and was typical of modern Japan in a state of change. he was most adamant that Japan must regain its status as a great international power, and he understood that this would mean complete industrialization. At the same time he wanted Japan to remain Asian in philosophy and way of life.

He loved the little things, the simple beauty, the peace of the inner life; he yearned for the kimono, though he saw the impracticability of this in a modern office. He loved the acres of gardens, but saw the need to use every available inch of land to improve living conditions and for the construction of giant buildings to deal with the ever-increasing population problem and the demands of the world market. He worshiped the ancient arts of archery, Judo, flower arrangement, classical dance and the tea ceremony, but he also felt the need to bounce with rock and roll. He was a mass of contradictions and he knew it. He was amazed and delighted with my knowledge of the ancient arts and culture of his country and appalled by my ignorance of modern industrial Japan.

"Imagine quiet gardens in the Ginza!"

Before we parted, we made arrangements to meet again

the following day. He planned to take me to visit the Judo Institute.

Tokyo's Judo Institute is a mammoth structure, a mass of training rooms, stairs, hallways with glass-like polished floors leading to observation galleries, lockers and showers. Men and boys of all ages move lightly through the building, each identifiable in terms of skill by his belt. They ranged from beginner to champion with all the gradations between.

When Abe-san appeared, his small waist was encircled with the belt of a champion.

There were no pre-arranged bouts; one looked about for an equal and, with only a nod, challenged him. Abe went about the large room, watching, challenging, matching his skills with others. His ability was obvious. He was fast, alert, lithe, sensitive to each move and powerful. Every encounter was performed with great ceremony, characterisic of the practiced art which Judo is. At the end of each bout, Abe-san would turn to me, with a wide smile, before returning to the task at hand which took his complete concentration.

As we walked to the shower rooms Abe said, "You must learn Judo. It makes one feel one's self."

The language classes continued to be an adventure. The students were more relaxed at each meeting. I planned the sessions with particular goals in mind: conversations about the home, the business, the garden, the visitor, the school, the city, directions and so on. For half of the period we would discuss the pronunciation of words and the correction of defective consonant sounds which the Japanese find so difficult: "th," "r," "l." For the remainder of the session, the students were free to bring in their own questions. I fully expected simple questions of grammar and word order. The questions were always well prepared, memorized with great care and quite impossible for me to answer.

"Doctor, please be so kind as to tell us. Why is it that

it is not all right for Russia to have missile bases in Cuba, because it is too close to the United States; but on the other hand it is all right for the United States to have missile bases in Japan, which is not too much further from Russia?"

"Doctor, do you believe it ethically right for a country to maintain its position through power; for example, money and bombs of great destructive potential?"

"Doctor, do you think that communism can be kept out of Asia? I speak of Chinese communism as contrasted to Russian communism."

These questions were asked with a sincere desire to know and without malice. Each was sufficient to bring about enough conversation for the remainder of the time allotted, as well as our usual several hour adjournment over cold beer.

One Sunday, Abe-san suggested that I meet him in Yokohama for a visit to the famous Susenski garden. He was waiting for me when I arrived at the station. He had removed his Western garb and looked superb in a long beige kimono and getas. We took a tram and descended on a narrow paved road through the outskirts of the city. The road was lined with tiny wooden homes, simple and beautiful in design, which were typical of those one sees everywhere in Japan.

The garden was enchanting with its tea houses, wooden bridges, twisted bonsai and blooming azaleas. In the rear of the garden was an authentic sixteenth-century farm house, complete with open fireplace, tatami, movable panel walls, finely constructed stairways. It was late afternoon and most of the visitors were gone. We removed our shoes and entered. We sat in an open section which looked out over the green at bamboo patches, tiny lakes and waterfalls.

"This is the Japan I love," Abe said softly. "It worries me that we are now in a position where to survive and compete with the rest of the world, we must become like it, which means that we must be willing to give up all of this and the wonders of our past. It is a difficult decision to make. This is a problem that we are not yet ready to solve. My parents see what is happening, but know that they can do nothing about it, so they retreat into the past which is familiar and, in small ways, fight the future. I see the advantages of the future, but I resist parting with the past."

He looked for a long time at the garden. "If this is all gone, we shall be like everyone else. Then where shall we go for quiet?"

Abe-san had made arrangements to take me to his home. The house was hidden behind the usual high wooden fence, on a quiet dirt road. A small gate led us into the garden. Moss covered the ground. There were small bonsai and a rather large fish pond where several golden and orange fish swam noiselessly. The only sound was the quiet splash of a small waterfall which ran over a few well-placed stones into a pond. I stood for a moment and watched.

Abe-san's mother and father (both in kimonos) walked out onto the open goza-covered porch from which the screens had been pushed back and bowed to us. We bowed back and were welcomed into the house. We entered a twelve-mat room (Sizes of rooms in Japan are determined by the number of tatami mats they contain.) There were three solid walls and one sliding wall by the garden which served as the entrance. The ceiling was low and there was little furniture—a few lacquered tables and a small Takonoma. The walls were bare except for a large scroll of calligraphy which hung above a beautiful classic flower arrangement of three simple flowers in the leafy branch of a maple tree.

I was given a pillow from a pile in one corner and knelt down with my hosts. Abe's mother and father spoke no English. His mother busied herself with a large hibachi and some water in a heavy brass pot.

"My mother is going to do a tea ceremony. She is very good with tea, a master," Abe told me.

We settled ourselves, after a short while, in a straight line, each on his own pillow. Abe's mother, looking very serene and beautiful, placed each coal in its proper position with long-pointed sticks. This done, she took the huge pot of water and set it on the coals. We waited for some time, listening to the sound of water beginning to boil and to the sounds of nature outside. The noise of a flapping fish tail in the pond seemed magnified ten-fold in the silence.

The tea implements were set before us, each of exquisite beauty and each in its proper place. With practiced strokes Abe's mother went through the ceremony: the measuring of the green tea, the pouring of the water, the quiet mixing, the wiping of the implements. All seemed to put us into a trance. At last she offered the first cup of tea to her husband who had quickly moved to her side. He passed it to me, and showed me how to take the cup, how to move it to the correct position so that I could see its design at best advantage, and how to drink the tea. He gave me a very sweet cookie which Abe explained was necessary to neutralize the tea's rather bitter taste.

During the ceremony a young girl—Abe's sister—entered and quietly seated herself next to him. She wore a brightly-colored kimono with a golden sash; her hair was cut in the usual schoolgirl fashion, with long bangs over her forehead. She was offered tea, after Abe had finished his; then the parents drank theirs and the ceremony was over. It seemed that it had been a matter of a few minutes and I was amazed to find that it had taken over an hour. Abe explained that the length of the tea ceremony is dictated by the mood. Some are brief, as nature and feelings do not commune, while others may last for hours when all is in tune.

I rose from my pillow with much effort. My cramped legs occasioned much laughter and comment.

The rest of the afternoon was spent in pleasant conversation, with Abe translating for his parents and sister. His sister was learning flower arranging and had done the arrangement now in the room.

Dusk in the garden was exquisite and I well understood Abe-san's reluctance to part with such beauty.

During my remaining weeks in Tokyo, I visited many families and found that most maintained the old traditions in their homes. There was great respect for the family. Each house, no matter how poor or how rich, had a unique beauty, always simple, plain and amazingly in tune with its natural setting.

The people were wondrous. There was Mrs. Hito who taught classic dance, who herself always seemed to be in a graceful dance position. There was Mrs. Ono who practiced the ancient art of weaving silk materials of great beauty. And Tomoyo whose job it was to take care of me at my inn. She was always waiting up no matter how late I returned and saw to it that my bath was never too hot, serving me at the moment of my request with great ease and beauty. She taught me patiently, and with constant ripples of laughter, how to eat, how to bathe. Then there was Fumio, educated in the United States, who had returned to Japan more determined than ever never to lose its spirit. These and many others just as wonderful made up the world of Japan in which I was still such a child.

With the aid of my friends, I made out a complete list of cities, towns and villages to be experienced and was ready to leave Tokyo.

The class gave me a farewell party at a most elegant Japanese-style restaurant, and escorted me, *en masse*, to the train.

As I left the station I thought I was beginning to see a possible answer. Tradition, the ingrained teachings of centuries, is not an easy thing to eradicate. Perhaps a compromise would be reached. The necessity of growth and the obvious advantages of improvements and modernization were weighed on one hand against the traditions of beauty, quiet, peace and individuality on the other. Could they be amalgamated?

Japan would find an answer in its own wise way. Abe had stated the problem: "If this is all gone, we shall be like everyone else. Then where shall we go for quiet?"

chapter 3

Hong Kong

As long as we have hope, we have direction, the energy to move, and the map to move by. We have a hundred alternatives, a thousand paths and an infinity of dreams. Hope-ful, we are half-way to where we want to go; hope-less, we are lost forever.

Wong

A few hours after arriving in Hong Kong, I met a spindly, pale, soft-spoken Chinese boy. His name was Wong; he was nineteen years old. I had come to see the sunset over the bay and found him seated beside a railing overlooking the harbor. He sat quietly, apparently oblivious of the noisy crowds that hurried to and from the Star Ferry, ready to cross from Hong Kong to its sister city, Kowloon.

Wong worked in a small toy shop twelve hours each day, starting at dawn and finishing just before sundown. Even so, he was able to wander each afternoon to the Kowloon ferry landing in time to watch the sunset.

I noticed that he fondled a small, well-worn Chinese-English dictionary.

"Do you speak English?"

"A little," he replied shyly. "Now, I teach myself. Soon maybe study in school. I have no chance for practice. To learn language one must practice." After some conversation

27

and with much effort he added, "You teacher. You teach English me, I teach Hong Kong."

Thus our friendship started. Through Wong a terrible world opened up before me with Hong Kong as the backdrop before which a battle for the maintenance of man's dignity was enacted each second by unsuspecting amateurs before a hard and indifferent audience.

With Wong as my guide, the several cities of Hong Kong, laid out amid ocean, rugged hills and lush New Territories began to unfold. The first city was that of fantastic shops, opulent hotels, gourmet restaurants, rich mansions, colorful tree-lined avenues and handsome people.

Another city was that of the business world, of money-hungry, desperate executives who measured wealth by the dividend and success by the profit, of the white-collar worker who in the most modern office buildings worked in air-conditioned panic on the world market, with all the anxieties of a New York commuter.

There was the city of the middle-class merchant who depended upon the throngs of tourists for his livelihood; who ran a small novelty shop, restaurant, a well-kept hotel or spotless tearoom.

Abhorred by the wealthy, ingored by the middle class, hidden from the casual observer and inconceivable to the simple tourist was the city of the refugee. This was Wong's city. A place of pride and poverty hidden behind the papier-mâché and glitter of Hong Kong glamour. Introducing me to the many-faceted city was Wong's part of the bargain.

My part of the agreement, to teach Wong English, began with evening walks of incredible variety. I taught him language of the street by way of the waterfront world of Suzy Wong, with its blaring night bars, and narrow alleys lined with street stalls and prostitutes; the language of the beautiful by gazing into windows alive with jewels from Europe, diamonds from Africa, trinkets from India, rugs from Persia, silks from Thailand; the language of money by way of the money changer—the French franc, the English pound, the American dollar, the Indian rupee, the Chinese yen. "Buy money with money." "Sell money with money." It was all handled in one simple transaction, with the speed and efficiency of an expert cook though with far less measured concern. Five dollars, four hundred, two thousand, forty thousand! We learned the vocabulary of travel by walking past miles of airline offices, steamship lines, tourist agencies, consulates, studios for passport pictures, offices of American Express and Diner's Club.

During our walks I learned more about Wong. There were ten other children in his family, all younger than he. They had been raised in Peking where their father was a well-to-do merchant until, to escape Communism, the family had left for Hong Kong and the home of a friend. When they arrived, the friend was compelled to turn them away; he had already used all of his resources to help the many others who had arrived before them. It was necessary, with their by then limited funds, to live in a small hotel until a permanent room could be found; but it was not long before they realized that finding a room was impossible in Hong Kong and were forced to take to the street or wherever they could find a plot of ground or temporary shelter. Money ran out and jobs were impossible to find; several members of the family became ill; a smaller brother died. Each move was to a place more desolate than the last until finally they were compelled to enter the dreaded refugee camp.

Each night after our wanderings, Wong accompanied me to my hotel. He seemed afraid to allow me to return alone. One night, as we approached Nathan Street through a small alleyway full of carts, bicycles, rickshaws and a million bodies in constant motion like jittery flies, he turned suddenly and asked, "Would you like to meet family of Wong?"

"Yes. Yes, I would."

"Sunday, at tea," he said, and after a quick, shy goodnight, he turned and walked briskly in the direction of his home.

On Sunday, we met at a small tea house near the port on the Kowloon side. Only Wong's mother, father and four older brothers came. We bowed to each other and sat down to tea. Wong acted as interpreter. Our conversation was simple and rather hesitant; we discussed the fact that I had never been to China, that I liked Hong Kong, that I was amazed at the number of people who lived in such a small area, and that I planned to remain for only a few more weeks. The brothers ate their food quietly with occasional shy glances in my direction. Wong's father had brought a gift for my mother, a small mandarin-style cotton house coat, obviously sewn by hand. There was embroidery on the collar and on the long, loose sleeves.

Wong's father told me how grateful he was for all that I was doing for his son. He felt it was important that all his family learn the language of their new home. Soon he would be making more coats like the one which he had given me for my mother and which was an original design. With the help of the entire family, he could supply the coats to a local merchant who was selling to tourists and English was imperative. Wong's father considered the present moment in Hong Kong a new world, a time to create anew, in whatever manner possible. It was no time for pride, self-pity or fear.

Much too quickly our tea was finished and, with bows, the family left.

Several days later Wong and I were wandering through the old section of Kowloon near the new multi-million dollar airport. The area was one of ragged beggars with frightened, fantastic faces. Its sky was composed of the converging tops of high, crumbling tenements and clotheslines where wash, strung like hanged phantoms, dangled and flapped in the breeze. As we neared the end of one street, Wong commented, "This is one of refugee places. It not seem part of Hong Kong." I looked at the area to which he was referring. It was a walled section—the wall, a patchwork of bits and pieces of cartons, tin, cardboard, piled stone and cement hunks, was shadowed by the surrounding ruined tenements. There were occasional small openings in the wall, just large enough for a human form to enter into what resembled a maze or labyrinth constructed of the same patchwork. It was a cubist's nightmare sketched in dull browns, hard grays and deep blacks.

"No law here. No police. Much bad and crime," Wong said, adding, "Will you see inside?"

We entered between crates, piled high. Wong knew his way and I followed. Only a discerning and practiced eye could have identified the proper directions. As we walked through the cardboard-box, tin-roof, broken-board community, slanted eyes sunken into drawn faces peered quietly at us. Here there was an almost ghostly stillness. Everyone seemed huddled together in frightened groups as if there were no place to hide. Spindly children with bloated bellies ran naked over piles of garbage. Sad-looking women sat on dirt floors and looked through us with dead expressions. A mass of tiny girls approached, screaming as much to Wong as to me. They were child prostitutes, some of them not even nine years old. Their little fingers were covered with dirt; their overly-long dresses were torn, soiled and ragged; their little feet were black with soil, scabby and infested with sores; their voices were shrill and desperate—and they grabbed at our bodies with eager, knowing hands.

The dirt paths were endless, branching crookedly in all directions like long arthritic fingers. They were covered with puddles of strong-smelling urine, piles of feces—the delight of swarming flies—bits of dried vegetable rind, cobs and discarded open tins. The odors were so strong that they pierced the senses into a painful numbness. Everything appeared devastated, dead, senseless—void of color or life. Adult prostitutes with still youthful bodies compressed within tight-fitting, sweat-stained mandarin dresses stood against paper walls without smiles and solicited sexlessly. Once beautiful faces were now masks, expressionless, blanched, untinged. The strong sweet smell of opium, mixed with the fumes of fires, dung, spoiled food and garbage, clouded the air.

Sometime later settled safely in a tearoom, I turned to Wong. I was stunned, speechless.

"There is no place else," Wong said simply.

"Who are those people?"

His answer was a whisper, "That is where I live."

Wong stayed with me that long night. We sat quietly in the dark of my noisy hotel room. I remember that during the evening he said, "Do not be sad. We work to find good life again. We work to make beautiful."

I wondered what there was about life so precious that a living horror was valued more highly than the peace of death. Perhaps what Wong said was true. Perhaps each man had his unconscious dream of beauty to which he strived and he will endure hunger, pain and untold suffering and degradation for its realization. Perhaps this dream was Wong's only reality. Perhaps only through his dream could he continue to feel and to believe in something. From dreams, changes can be made.

Wong told me that the government was building apartments but the waiting lists were long and the houses were filled beyond capacity before they were even completed. Greedy landlords were charging high prices for hovels, which could only be afforded if several families moved in together, making the situation little better.

My last few days in Hong Kong were spent enrolling Wong in a good night school for English lessons and supplying him with books on English grammar and conversation.

It was not an easy thing to leave Wong. He was so much more than nineteen years old: proud, independent, gentle, affectionate, kind and responsive. The day I left he met me at the airport. He had taken the day off from work and was waiting for me. I went through all the necessary formalities without looking at him until we retired with a cup of tea to a corner of the luxurious coffee shop. The atmosphere was unreal as if we suddenly had become strangers, as if we had revealed ourselves too completely and now were ashamed. It was as if we somehow had to recover ourselves, to replace the facades which protected us against nakedness and guilt. At last Wong spoke.

"Will some day you come back to Hong Kong?"

"I hope so. I don't know."

"I not write English too well. I study much. Someday I repay you for nice things you do for me and family. You will see."

The plane was called. We embraced.

"I bring you present," Wong said, and handed me a tiny package. "It is a little package, but a big gift. You open on airplane, please. Do you know where I go tonight?" he asked as I started to the gate. "I go to Star Ferry where I meet you. I watch sunset."

I boarded the plane, and with superjet efficiency was off and overlooking the faint outline of Hong Kong on the sea.

I took out Wong's gift and opened it. It was a small Buddha. The Buddha was fat and smiling.

I leaned back in my seat and thought of Wong. I could clearly see his thin body seated quietly on a bench amid the frantic pre-dinner rush at the Star Ferry, his drawn, sad, rather pale face and his shining eyes, orange in the sunset. I put the Buddha in my jacket pocket.

Strange, but I felt good.

chapter 4

Thailand

To deny ourselves the knowledge even of a single person is to lose the central piece of the jigsaw puzzle.

Kanoke

Thailand is virtually unique among the countries of Asia. Its people have never known colonization, mass hunger or oppression. They are prosperous, relaxed and happy.

Bangkok, the capital of Thailand, stands like an Oriental Disneyland. Its hundreds of temples are exotic, each one unique. Their grand, colorful silhouettes can be seen for miles spreading across the horizon.

The Chao Phraya River runs through the city like a jade snake pin. From it, canals jet out like the sticks of a fan forming colorful islands. These islands keep the city alive with activity and form the famous floating markets.

The entire city is surrounded with marshy rice fields, added security against poverty.

With the temples, the islands, the more than four hundred exotic monasteries, the towering Royal Palace with its vast chambers in silk and velvet, Bangkok turns the ancient tales of the gold-laden Orient into reality.

This is the land of the Reclining Buddha, the shaved-headed, saffron-robed Buddhist, and the powerful cemented Roc.

There are fairs, carnivals and religious holidays aplenty to keep the fun-loving people happy as well as a spring-like atmosphere between festivals to keep them active. The Thai have the reputation of being the friendliest and most hospitable people in Asia, and they have created an ideal setting in which to enjoy these gifts.

For the tourist, the city is a heaven. Transportation is cheap and efficient. Hotels are ultra-modern and offer every convenience. Restaurants serve Oriental and Western foods with equal ease, cooked to vie with the best anywhere in the world. There are bars with blaring jukeboxes where one can sit in air-conditioned comfort and sip dry martinis prepared to taste. Coffee houses prepare Maxwell House in electric percolators or espresso in giant machines. One can shop in opulent surroundings, buy silks of any length, style or color desired. If what you seek is not displayed, it can be made to order and delivered to your hotel within hours.

Bangkok offers pleasures of a different, more modest nature for those who cannot afford first class, pools and air-conditioned comfort. There are hotels, shops and restaurants to suit any budget. These can be found down most side streets or alleyways.

A lean budget and sparse accommodations compelled me to share the luxuries of such a hotel with another gentleman, an American salesman. The hotel was a small wooden structure in what seemed to be a patio behind a series of business establishments which lined a main street. Our tiny, neat room was equipped with two wrought-iron beds, each with a sagging, lumpy innerspring mattress, one window and a sink marked with hot and cold spigots from which you could always be assured of a full supply of cold water, whichever spigot you tried. In addition, and at no extra charge, the guests were treated to several varieties of bugs, a small temperamental fan which usually did not work and, on the hotel gounds, a noisy bar with several available prostitutes.

The management was always ready to smile, to listen, to nod about such complaints as "There's some sort of animal on the ceiling," "The door doesn't close," "Could you please ask the fat prostitute to stop coming into my room." But nothing was ever done.

Mack, my roommate, was in his late forties. He did not seem to be bothered by any of these small inconveniences. "Hell," he would say, "this ain't the Waldorf Astoria. Anyway, I save money this way. I like it here. I can't stand those damn tourist hotels full of virgin schoolteachers and their damn guidebooks."

Mack was tall, husky, fair-skinned and blond, the physical type best loved and immediately recognized by the Asian as American. He had been in Bangkok several times on business trips for his U.S.-based pharmaceutical firm.

"This is quite a place, Bangkok. That Buddha and the Palace are real nice but the best things are the dames. I know plenty of 'em, kid. Sexy, cheap and clean. Say the word and I can fix you up."

"What the hell ya wanna travel here for, anyway, kid? Me? I take care of my business, play around a little after hours and get the hell out."

On the first evening I spent with Mack, he took me to a Western-style restaurant. "Damn good American food," he assured me. "You've got to stay away from that Thai crap unless you want to get the creeping 'dingle dangle.'"

After dinner he took me to a bar near the river. "I get a real kick outta this place," he chuckled. His entrance caused quite a stir.

"Mack, my honey!" the women swarmed to him. "Mack, my stud! My bull!"

He received them with obscene gestures, slapped them on their fat bottoms and exclaimed, "Now, ain't she something? And a tiger in bed!"

He pulled a rather fleshy woman in our direction and pushed her at me. "Feel," he smiled, "Smell. Doesn't she have it all over them Indian whores?"

The woman reeked of a rather cheap flower perfume. She did not move but struck what she imagined as a provocative pose right out of a Harlow movie which I found wonderfully amusing though I hesitated to smile for fear it be misinterpreted.

"Really something," Mack said and slapped her backside. "Plenty for your money, too. Want it?"

It was apparent that our taste in both women and travel was quite different. Many evenings Mack didn't return and I was often gone before he showed up in the morning. I could tell when he had been there, as the room was always strewn with the clothes he left about in his rush to get to work.

When he departed after a week, the hotel manager approached me meekly to ask if I would mind sharing my room with a Thai gentleman.

"He's a clean, young businessman," the manager assured me. "One of our steady customers."

I told him I wouldn't mind.

In this way Pricha and I were introduced. He was a small man in his late twenties, dark, thin and pleasant looking. His clothing was neat and conservative; his manner was straightforward and formal. "My name is Pricha," he introduced himself. "I am Thai."

It soon became a habit for us to have dinner together. We went often to a small Thai restaurant on Chak Ching

Road, where he was known and ate fantastically exotic and delicious foods. Since Pricha was aware of everything about him and seemed to be able to literally "smell out" the excitement in the city, there was never a problem as to where we would spend the evening, be it a Chinese opera, a carnival or a new street magician.

After dinner one evening, Pricha suggested that we take a boat trip on the river. He explained that the real beauty of the great river and the floating market section was to be seen at night. We went to a small dock off a side street where several sampans about the size of Venetian gondolas were tossing about in the river. Pricha requested a boat and we were at once deluged with offers of various prices. He finally selected a sampan owned by a rather young boy, more pleasant and less aggressive than the other boatmen. Then Pricha walked to a food stand to purchase several items while the boy lit a small lantern and waited, smiling at me warmly. We pushed off into the river and almost at once the boat was caught by the current and pulled quietly downstream.

The city's thousands of colored lights were reflected at our feet in a shimmering watery blur. The large temples bordering the river now resembled giant black monsters hovering over us, ready to strike and devour. All the gaudiness and color of the daytime Bangkok was now but an Oriental shadow play, dark and graceful.

The night was warm and the lamb and chicken which Pricha had bought tasted good even on a full stomach. He had purchased several bottles of beer which we shared with our boatman. The only sound was that of the oars gliding through the water. The lantern flickered continuously.

The beer was potent and soon the silence was broken by the boatman's lusty singing. His repertoire, made up mostly of Western songs which he sang in a relaxed pidgin English, was delightful and pleasant. "Don' ya' nose . . ." We could not help but laugh.

As we passed through narrow canals cutting through the lush, nearly deserted market district, we could see the many occupants of the floating town going about the business of living, laughing gaily. Small groups of people stood chatting, arguing or listening intently.

At one point, Pricha asked the boatman to stop.

"Since you are interested in people, shall we rest here awhile?" He was referring to what looked like a small inn floating on a marshy island. Inside, the room was filled with men, smoke and the smell of beer.

"So the workman spends his nights like workmen all over the world I suppose, with friends, a cigarette and a bottle of beer," I thought.

The group greeted Pricha with a friendly welcome, though they obviously did not know him. They surveyed me oddly but immediately included me in the circle on the floor.

After so many days, Pricha and I had become fast friends. He told me of his family and friends, of his dreams for the future and his fears. His dreams were simple like those of any man, anywhere; his fears were rather unique but none the less real, understandable and human.

After a week, Pricha made plans to visit some of his relatives, farmers who lived a very different kind of life from that which I had seen so far in Bangkok. He asked if I cared to go with him.

"They are not poor people," he said proudly. "They have fields of rice, only their lives are more simple than ours."

We took a crowded, noisy streetcar from our hotel and then a bus to the end of the line. We were more than an hour's drive from the center of Bangkok, which had faded to a dim glow on the horizon. At the end of the bus line were several small cars, old retired taxis, repaired to run an additional million miles, again serving their original function outside the city from which they had been outlawed. For some time Pricha talked with several drivers, obviously concerned about the price and our destination. When everything was finally arranged, we climbed into one of the ancient cars and started off in a rumble down a dirt road.

Abruptly, the road came to an end in the midst of moonlit rice paddies. The tall rice plants hid the muddy water below which slushed mysteriously, unseen in the dark.

"From here we must walk," Pricha informed me. "The taxi will wait for us. I think it would be wise for you to remove your shoes, socks and trousers. We shall have to walk on wet, slippery boards in the dark. You are likely to step into the mud now and then and it will be better if you don't get your clothes ruined." I did as he suggested and we started off down the planks which—edged occasionally by a single, weakly constructed handrail—seemed to lead nowhere. There was neither light nor house in sight.

It was much like walking a blind maze. Pricha led and I followed close behind, one hand on the rail and the other on his shoulder as he had instructed.

The planks were jagged and veered first to one side, then the other. I could feel the mud push its slimy way between my toes and the tops of the rice plants brush against my ankles. We attracted thousands of insects. I neither dared nor cared to stop for even a moment. I was afraid to let go of Pricha or the rail to swat them. Rather than let go, I allowed them to bite and suck away.

Several times we came upon a fork with planks going in two directions, but Pricha always knew without hesitation which branch to follow.

The walk was much farther than I had imagined. At last, seemingly growing out of a rice swamp and completely surrounded by it, there emerged a cluster of small wooden shacks, scattered about on what appeared to be a tiny island.

Pricha called out, "Kanoke!"

In a moment, a young man draped only with a white cloth about his slim waist emerged from one of the shacks and stood momentarily silhouetted in the dimly lit doorway.

"Kanoke! It's me, Pricha," he seemed to be saying.

The young man, obviously delighted, approached with open arms to plant a kiss on Pricha's mouth. Pricha introduced us. He could not speak English, but I was surely welcome for he kissed me firmly on the mouth just as he had his relative.

He led us into the shack, lit with a single oil lamp. The room was empty except for some farming tools and a few open bed rolls. There were two windows which were closed to the night and a mat in the center of the floor on which we sat, almost in darkness.

The two men spoke quickly and at once. There was great warmth and animation in their conversation. At last it occurred to Kanoke that I was being excluded. He reached out and took my hand warmly in his. His hand felt rough and strong.

"He regrets that he cannot speak to you," Pricha translated. "He wants to awaken his family to have you meet them, but I will not allow it. They work very hard all day and would be very tired."

Kanoke rose and started for the door. He took the lamp in his hand and motioned for us to follow him. "He insists that you at least see them," Pricha said. "He's very proud of his family."

We walked out into the night which now seemed a bit lighter. The fields of rice which surrounded us were vast and silent and only the glow in the sky from the distant city reminded me that we were still part of this century.

Kanoke walked directly to a small shack and opened the door. With the candle, he lit up the faces and relaxed, sleeping bodies of several children. None of them stirred. Their expressions were soft, peaceful. In another room, a short distance away were two older boys in their early teens. Their bare shoulders and chests were exposed, strong, dark and firm. One of the boys sat up slightly and spoke, but with the assurance of his father's response, lay back and seemed to fall asleep again instantaneously.

Kanoke looked proudly at me and smiled.

At last we met his wife. She looked like one of the children, youthful and shy. She wore a loose-flowing petticoat; her feet and ankles were bare.

She busied herself at once, fixing tea with quick, sure movements.

For a long while we sat outside in the now friendly darkness, drank the hot tea and ate small rice cakes. Pricha and Kanoke spoke in soft tones.

When the time came to leave, Kanoke insisted upon walking back with us over the long-planked path to the road. Pricha guided me from the front and Kanoke supported me from the rear. I was, indeed, well guarded from everything except the insects that feasted themselves greedily on my still unhardened skin.

When we arrived at the road, Kanoke led us to a trough where we could wash the mud from our feet and legs. The taxi driver, who had fallen asleep at the wheel, seemed a bit disappointed and annoyed that we had returned so soon.

Kanoke kissed us both with great tenderness. He looked at me deeply, smiled nodding his head from side to side approvingly, and then impulsively kissed me again.

We left Kanoke in the soft darkness of his strange world and started back to town.

"He is a fine man. He liked you very much," Pricha said.

"He felt that you were comfortable in his home. You are the first Westerner he has ever known. You have given him great honor."

All at once I thought of Mack, loud, insensitive, rough. How sad that he would never known Kanoke's kiss.

chapter 5

Cambodia

We will find the greatest riches where we find the joy in living; since we serve God and ourselves best in joy, it seems to be the only sensible goal in life.

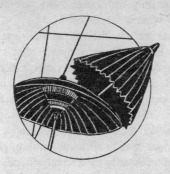

Hotel de la Paix

Phnom-Penh is the Asian city of the Emerald Buddha, with a dash of France, her colonizer. Large, graceful temples lining the horizon; spicy-smelling marketplaces selling everything from cheap images of the Buddha to Chanel No. 5 and Gillette Blue Blades; dark-skinned natives cycling quickly through congested, dirty streets; and nearby the great river rushing through the city, teeming with activity; all this is Phnom-Penh.

It is a full day's bus trip from Phnom-Penh to Siem Reap. The native bus is open to the elements, has wooden seats, stops any time for everyone and everything and is, in spite of this, quite reliable.

We left Phnom-Penh at dawn when it was still cool. I had packed a small lunch of French bread, cheese and fresh fruit as I had learned that there were no such things as lunch shops and no schedules to advise the traveler when the trip would end. When I inquired about time schedules, my questions were met only with queer looks, grunts, groans and "me no know what is schedules!"

At dawn, as we left, the streets were just beginning to take on life. Bicycles were standing idle; sweepers who tried continuously to keep the roads clean pushed their brooms along in tired, steady rhythms, as if they knew it was in vain; shopkeepers sleepily opened their shutters.

The bus passed through these morning rituals with quick indifference and left the city. Almost at once we were plunged into jungle which was to surround us throughout the trip, broken only momentarily by a small village, a stream or a river.

The seats on the bus were all reserved, but this did not include those passengers who were standing or hanging on outside. The luggage was tied high on the roof, like a pyramid of multi-colored, odd shapes. I was seated next to the only other person on the bus who was not a native. She was a short, severely dressed, neatly groomed woman. Her face was small with delicate features, except for her lips which were full and well shaped. She wore a skirt and blouse, both gray, well pressed and clean. Obviously, she was not a fellow tourist, usually recognizable by the wash-and-wear quality of the press in his clothes and the tense, almost pathetically lost quality of his expression.

I introduced myself. "Would you rather sit by the window?" I asked.

She thanked me, "No. I have been on this road many times. It is a lovely drive, but I am sure that you will enjoy the window more than I. I am Madame Clote. I live in Siem Reap."

I explained, during the drive, that I understood there were two luxury hotels in Siem Reap, both very good, but very expensive and far beyond my means. I had heard also of a third hotel which was much cheaper but quite nice.

She knew the hotel about which I spoke, "The Hôtel de la Paix." Yes, it was located in the city itself, quite some way from the ruins of Angkor which she assumed I had come to see. "Why else would someone go to Siem Reap?" She smiled. "I am surprised that you spent time in Phnom-Penh. To the Western world, except for a few of us who have lived here for many years and love it, Cambodia is just a vast jungle of uncivilized people with nothing to recommend it but the massive ruins of ancient Angkor."

We talked for some time. I was embarrassed to learn that she and her husband were the proprietors of the city's most expensive and most coveted hotel. She did not seem at all disturbed but rather amused by my discussion of expensive hotels, commenting, "One pays for quality—even in the jungle."

She, too, had brought food and combining our lunches we had quite a feast. She supplied a bottle of wine, a real necessity as the heat of the day increased. The wine, the food, the heat and the swaying of the bus lulled us into afternoon naps. When we awoke we were entering Siem Reap. It seemed more colorful, less congested and less dusty than Phnom-Penh.

Madame directed me to the hotel which was just a few hundred feet from the bus station, and I saw her step into a large, chauffeur-driven car which drove off in a spray of dust.

Alone, I was immediately pounced upon by several bicycle drivers, all wearing variations of a small pair of shorts, usually too large to be held up by their flat bellies and narrow hips, always ready to fall about them on the ground.

"I take you to ruins," they all shouted in perfect English.

"You come with me."

"I take you cheap."

"I be your guide."

"I'm going to the Hôtel de la Paix," I said.

They seemed confused. Obviously, this was not a part of their practiced dialogue. They looked from one to the other, then followed in silence.

The Hôtel de la Paix was a rather small, box-like, two-story stucco structure. The lower level was partially devoted to a large restaurant and, outside, there was a four-table sidewalk cafe. The sign on the wall was broken and read, "Hôt de . . ."

"Oui," said the proprietor, who spoke only French, "Nous avons une chambre."

He took me up the flight of stairs into a narrow hall. My room was at the far end, with windows on two sides. One, facing the rear of the hotel, overlooked the yard of a very large, very noisy native family and their menagerie of chickens, cows, pigs, motor scooters and children. The other window looked across a mucky field to the dense jungle which vied successfully with the yard for animal noises.

There was a small, single bed with a torn mosquito net hanging loosely over it, a dresser and a table. The toilet had a basin, shower and commode, all crowded together in a space so cramped that one could perform all functions with hardly a move of the body.

"Très jolie, n'est pas?" the proprietor beamed.

I took the room, together with two meals, for a dollar and a half a day. A good price, indeed, I thought.

After my first night I was not so certain. The native family seemed to be having a perpetual orgy with a record player screaming out into the night, obviously not only amusing the many guests but also delighting the animals that answered in their own spirited tones. Women laughed, children cried, men argued. Each spoke as if everyone else were deaf.

It was no better inside the hotel. The hallway was like

the Rue de la Paix for which the hotel was named. Doors
opened with creaking sounds and slammed shut. Men whis-
pered loudly, women giggled and screeched with joy. Feet
pattered, objects fell and windows crashed.

At one point, there was a loud knock at my door.

"Who is it?" I asked angrily.

The knock was repeated. I rose, put a shirt over my
sweaty nakedness and answered the door. A very young
girl, not over fifteen, pushed her way into the room. Her
garbled French was incomprehensible, but her purpose was
obvious.

After much discussion, none of which she understood,
I had to remove her bodily from the room, cursing myself
for having fallen into this age-old trap, so common among
Asian prostitutes.

When I finally fell asleep it was almost morning.

The sun was already unbearably hot when I awoke and
light was pouring through the shadeless windows. I struggled through my morning ritual, the cold water actually
feeling good over my tired, insect-drained flesh. Finally, I
got myself downstairs for breakfast.

The proprietor was busily packing things in an old fash-
ioned ice box.

"Bonjour," he said. "Et alors?"

I mentioned that there certainly had been a great deal of
noise during the night.

"Oui," he smiled, "c'est merveilleux!"

The manager directed me to the ruins. He advised me
about bargaining with the cyclists and motorbike drivers and
felt that for no more than two dollars I should be able to
hire one for the day. They could take me on a pre-planned
tour which included La Grande Cercle, Angkor Wat and
some of the major sights and La Petite Cercle, some of the
more remote ruins. This, he felt, I could see in two days;

if I wanted to really see and feel it, it would take five; while if I wanted to see, feel and perceive, it might take a lifetime.

He went out and hired a motorbike. The driver was a spindly boy whose half-naked body appeared dried by the sun. His head seemed too large for his thin frame, but he had a pleasant face, soft and peaceful. I liked him. He spoke only a few words of English and a few more of French, but I felt sure that we would be able to communicate adequately for the relationship we would be having in Angkor. His name sounded like Noke.

After breakfast of good hot café au lait and fresh French bread, I piled into the buggy. The motorbike sputtered and spat as we left in a cloud of dust, with Noke smiling broadly in front of me.

It was a wonderful morning. The sky was clear and a deep blue. The jungle looked rich and dense, like a fantasy land.

Noke pointed out one of the modern hotels. It was white, tall, well-kept. The gardens were beautiful and full of colorful tropical flowers. Well-dressed, camera-carrying tourists sat about the veranda reading, talking or simply staring at the large open space around the hotel.

"Much francs," Noke said as we sputtered by. Cars were waiting in front of the hotel to take the guests to the ruins in cool comfort. "Why you no stay there?"

"No francs," I answered. He laughed, "Moi aussi."

We traveled dustily down the narrow main road, completely lined with giant trees and shrubs, alive with the high-pitched screech of insects. At the end of the road, bathed in the hot mid-morning sun, stood the great side gate of Angkor Wat. A large staircase poured down into a vast, moss-flower, insect-infested moat. The walls extended almost endlessly on either side. Towers, stairways and paths made interesting patterns against the skyline and gave steady support to hungry vines and bushes.

The main entrance was tremendous and led to the vast central sanctuary through several walls, magnificent gates and courts within courts. All along the stone walkway were exquisitely carved sacred naga serpents, menacingly guarding the sanctuary—a central group of rooms and towers of beautiful symmetry and giant size.

In the afternoon sun, Angkor Wat turns orange and seems like a jewel set carefully in a wild jungle setting. Undisturbed, one can sit for hours on one of the central towers, high above the complex of buildings and view a city which, though built in the 12th century, was being eaten by the jungle, slowly and hungrily, until only a century ago. Here, the Khmer Empire blossomed for some 600 years, rich and exciting, creating artistic and architectural masterpieces with hordes of slaves. Vast irrigation systems were set up, great cities of incomparable beauty flourished in the shadow of overpoweringly lovely temples protected by the seven-headed naga. Then suddenly, inexplicably, all was seized by the jungle's hungry fingers; it was all hidden, vanished.

Angkor Wat is only one of hundreds of monuments and temples covering an area of six hundred square kilometers. Awesome, magnificent, defying time and jungle, they remain almost intact and allow modern man a chance to glimpse a vanished civilization and bask in its mystery.

The hordes of tourists were disconcerting: grumbling about the heat, the endless steps and the vastness of the city; dashing through the fantastic setting, hurrying to make it fit within a one- or two-day itinerary. However, time did not permit them to remain too long in any one place, and no sooner had their rumble and dash disturbed the peace than it moved on and out of earshot, leaving one to continue his journey in silence.

Saffron-robed priests from nearby Buddhist temples wandered quietly alone or in small groups through the temples and gazed at the fantasy of their past culture before returning to the simplicity of their tiny wooden temples, dwarfed and insignificant in comparison with these ancient buildings.

Madame's hotel was directly across the road from Angkor Wat. I walked in, looking for her, and was told that she was in the kitchen supervising the preparation of lunch. When she saw me she greeted me as an old friend. "How do you like your hotel?" she asked.

"Well," I answered, "there is very little 'Paix,' but I think it will be fine."

She laughed. "You are brave."

We talked for a few minutes, experiencing several interruptions. Her staff spoke both the native tongue and French.

"Madame, Mrs. Charles in Room 18 says her air-conditioning makes too much noise."

"Mr. and Mrs. Smith want to know if you have arranged for the station wagon so that they can go to Bantai Serei tomorrow."

"There is not enough coffee for lunch and dinner. We need more."

"Should I take the elephant out this afternoon? The children of the couple in Room 16 want to ride him and take pictures."

"Miss Barsi says the crickets are too loud."

"I must go," Madame said finally. "Come to dinner here tonight. I would like you to meet my husband and a few friends. Nine o'clock? Oh, yes, and you must visit Bantei Serei. I have a station wagon which takes my guests. It is too far for a motorbike. If there is an empty seat, I shall save it for you."

I waited that day to watch the temple turn a bright yellow-orange-red in the light of the setting sun. I wandered through its deep, heavy, ancient halls and then out onto a small path which led to the simple Buddhist monastery adjacent to the ruins. I thought I heard the sound of voices and laughter and, although the ruins seemed deserted, followed it up a large stone staircase to the top of a wall along the side of the moat which separated the ruins from the surrounding roads and jungle. The laughter and voices grew louder. Twenty or thirty young monks, heads shaved, naked bodies the color of the ancient walls, skin glistening in the orange light, were lying in the tall grass, splashing in the muddy water of the moat, running up and down the stairs with happy, boyish laughter and using tall stones, crumpled with age, as impromptu diving boards.

Unseen, I watched them for some time. I did not want to inhibit their spontaneity or dampen their joy. I could still hear their laughter as I re-entered the temple and started back to the motorbike which Noke had parked under a tree.

Returning to my hotel, I changed for dinner. When I explained to the manager that I would be eating at the Hôtel du Temple, he seemed rather disappointed. "We have much better food here than they do at the du Temple," he said. "There they wash out all the goodness and cook everything to death for the tourists who will not eat anything unless it's mush. You will see." He seemed sincerely hurt.

"I'll certainly eat here tomorrow," I assured him.

"I will have something special for you," he said.

Dinner at Madame's was excellent. I had been eating bread and cheese for so long that to have salad with oil and vinegar, fresh-made soup, chicken with potatoes and fresh vegetables, and real ice cream was a joy. The conversation was most exciting. I had revealed my intense desire to know the Cambodian people. My companions at dinner agreed that the Cambodians were certainly worth knowing, that they were warm people with a simple yet profound way of life.

One of the gentlemen present asked if I cared to meet a friend of his who lived on the lake. "Lake people have the true essence of the real Cambodian, untouched by either colonizer or tourist." I was delighted. Arrangements were made for me to bicycle to the lake and I was given a letter to the friend who spoke French fluently.

The next few days I spent with Noke puttering from one great wonder to another. The enchanting Ta Prohm, the mystery of Bayon, the glory of the Terraces of the Leper King and the Elephants—with its immense terraces and galleries topped with the two hundred colossal stone faces of the gods, serene, smiling and at peace whether in a thriving civilization, overrun by the jungle, or the object of the tourist gaze.

I took the long trip to Bantei Serei, the pink temple lost until 1914 from the gaze of man, and to the temples of Beng Mealea, Pheah Kahn and Koh Ker.

Each trip was full of wonder. Noke seemed proud, as if each temple belonged to him personally. He was free to show, reveal, defame or slander if he chose. With a true flare for the dramatic, he took the most glorious approaches through wild dense jungle, stopping here and there to reveal an area which as yet had not been excavated and which, he felt sure, was full of wonders even more fantastic than those we had been viewing.

After a week I set off on a borrowed motorbike along the river from Siem Reap to the lake. The Tonle Sap is a gigantic body of water covering about one-third of the territory of Cambodia. The river was one of the main tributaries. Life along the river was wonderful to watch. Small, well-built shacks with their water wheels, women washing, men and children bathing, vendors—all the things which made up the slow-paced life of the people who knew pretty generally what tomorrow would bring and were not too concerned about it.

I followed the river, as instructed, never leaving the main road. Soon I left the city behind and cycled for what seemed like hours through level brush-swamp country. Finally, in the distance I could see a tiny city of shacks on the shore of the lake. It was late afternoon. The fishing boats had returned and some of the men were working on them, while others were mending nets, large sacks or boxes. Several children came to greet me shouting with joy and puzzlement. The men continued to work, but obviously were aware of my presence. "Monsieur Gilwee?" I asked.

"Làbas," one of the men answered, and the others laughed at his use of French.

By this time a rather short, husky, middle-aged man with a thick crop of black hair hanging over his weathered face was walking toward me.

He spoke in flawless French: "My name is Gilwee."

I told him who had sent me and why and asked if this was a good time for a visit or if I had come in a very busy, inconvenient season.

"Now is always a good time. There is no bad time to welcome friends," he answered.

We moved down a dirt road which followed the shore of the lake. It was lined with small wooden shacks on tall posts that kept them standing high above the water. They all seemed to have only one room with open windows and to contain little furniture.

"Our life here is very simple. We fish, we plant small gardens, and we reap what we sow. When our catch is good we sell to the merchants who come from Siem Reap, but mostly they cheat us and it is not worth the trouble to sell the fish. The fish feed the people here and we must make sure that we do not allow the lake to become barren."

Gilwee's shack was like the others, small and empty, with one large window giving an unobstructed view of the giant lake and the tall masses of pussy willow lining the shore.

"It is truly beautiful, is it not?" It was a statement, not a question. "I hope you can stay for some time. You are very welcome here."

He took me out onto the lake in his small motor-propelled fishing boat. En route, we saw boats at anchor, and endless living. There were women squatted on buoys to wash the children in their arms. They smiled as we passed. Young boys paddled about in the muddy lake like pollywogs. The entire scene was movement.

When we had lost sight of the shore, Gilwee stopped the motor and let the boat float soundlessly in its own ripples. "This is our lake," he said simply. The sun was setting and the colors danced on the calm water. There was no sound except the occasional slap of a wave against the boat's side.

"In such calm it is hard to imagine that this lake becomes a demon during the monsoon. The waves are too high and dangerous for these tiny boats. Sometimes our houses are washed away and we must live together, depending on each other for our very lives. Each year's monsoon seems worse than the year before, but we know it is only our memory which forgets the unpleasant, remembering only moments like this." I sat back in the boat and listened to the silence.

The next few days were mostly spent in watching. I found it amazingly simple to be assimilated by the community. The children followed me everywhere, the men fought to have me in their boats or to invite me to join them at their work. Love and security were as apparent and refreshing as the cool breezes that blew off the lake and the fresh smell of the fish which were unloaded on the dirt road from the tiny boats.

Gilwee explained, "We seem to have nothing, but we have no use for anything more. Nature, when you live so close to her, tells you that there is no reason for things. Things are destroyed in storms and taken away from you. Feelings and knowledge and closeness with God are what we seek, for these are the only things which remain with us even in famine and flood or when all seems lost. We are Buddhists. These are the things we believe."

After a few days, I left. I had become attached to them, and they had enjoyed me. But there was no pain in leaving because somehow these people had been trained to hold on to nothing, for all things eventually must go.

When I returned to Siem Reap, I was already an old friend at the Hôtel de la Paix. The noise had long since ceased to bother me and busy days lulled me to sleep with their rich, vital experiences. The prostitute and her friends were constant dinner companions.

The meals at the La Paix were grand. Each day the manager posted a long list of what was to be served. He always went through the act of asking, "And what would you have today?" At first, I would examine the list carefully and he would announce, "The tripe is excellent today."

"I think I'll have the rabbit."

"I'm sorry but the rabbit is all gone."

"Then I'll have the coq au vin."

"It is gone, too."

"Well, then what do you suggest?"

He would brighten up, "The tripe is excellent."

"Then it will be the tripe."

Soon I understood that the list was a dream, that there was always one dish which one must allow him to suggest and then follow his suggestion. This presented no problem as the food was uniformly delicious.

On my last day, I said goodbye to all of my new friends at the Hôtel de la Paix. We exchanged addresses, then I climbed into the seat behind Noke who looked very sad. I had loved the hotel and felt a deep sense of losing something very real. In spite of the bites which covered my body, the strange nonexistent menu, and the not too efficient clean-up crew, the hotel had real charm, truly French Cambodian: not actually French, yet not Cambodian. It was something like the country, not poor and not rich, but proud, full of life and the love of life.

The little one-shack airport was bustling with tourists. The two or three Cambodian officials checked us through slowly with little concern about complaints and accusations of inefficiency. They were proud and polite, but left no doubt that Angkor was theirs. They could not be shouted at, bought or attacked. This, after all, was their country.

chapter 6

Saigon

We must learn to let go as easily as we grasp or we will find our hands full and our minds empty. Though every hello is the beginning of a goodbye, do not lose heart; for every goodbye may also be the beginning of another hello.

Lat

The he most fantastic thing about Saigon is its women. Neither Asian nor European, they have the best qualities of both cultures. They are small, well built, slim, graceful, feminine, literate and a joy to be with. Their dress is the most gracious in the world. They wear the ao dai, a tight sheath dress which flows to the ground, usually of a single color, pale blue, pink, green or yellow. A slit from the floor to above the hips allows the front and back panels to fall loosely and gracefully about them. Under the dress there is a pair of dark, loose-fitting, pajama-type silk trousers. On their feet they wear high heels. No sight is more lovely than watching one of these small, beautiful women riding on the back of a motor scooter, holding on to her boyfriend with her head tossed back, a smile on her face, hair tied neatly in place and the tail of her dress flapping loosely behind her in the wind.

Lat was such a girl. I first saw her from a distance as

she led four tourists through Saigon's giant zoo, pointing gracefully to this animal and that with the gestures of a dancer. As she approached I could hear the sing-song quality of her voice which sounded most pleasant. She was not over five feet tall and weighed no more than ninety pounds. Her hair and eyes were dark; her skin, a golden tan. She seemed to be constantly smiling.

"These are but a few of the Manu birds we have in Vietnam," I heard her say. "The colors are amazing, too, no?" She paused, giving the tourists an opportunity to inspect the birds, then added, "Now we will go to the snake section, perhaps the most interesting collection in Asia." To my surprise, she turned to me. "Have you seen the snake collection? It's just over there," she pointed.

"No, I haven't," I answered. "I'm going there next."

"Come with us, then," she said matter-of-factly. The group moved after her and I followed.

"Are you a tourist?" she asked.

"Yes."

"Alone?" She looked at me with large, almond-shaped eyes. "No tour?"

"No," I answered, "no tour, and, yes, alone."

She led us to the snake section and again began her melodious explanation. When she had finished, she backed away, allowing her group to take a closer look.

"They are beautiful, I think. Most people believe there is nothing so terrible as a reptile, but we grow up with them in Southeast Asia," she said. "Have you ever seen any so large or so colorful?"

"You are not a soldier?" she asked after a moment.

"No," I answered.

"I didn't think you were American at first. Americans seldom travel alone. I thought you must be French or even

Italian. Americans here are either soldiers or very old or schoolteachers. Which are you?"

She did not wait for an answer but turned to her group. "There is a refreshment stand over there and some benches by a lovely lake. Perhaps you would like to rest a few minutes before we go to the temple in the city."

The group seemed eager to comply with her suggestion and sauntered off with familiar dialogue . . .

"I'm tired!"

"I don't know why I came on this tour, anyway. An animal is an animal."

"She's cute, but it's too damn hot."

"Did you ever see so many god-awful snakes? I hate snakes!"

They vanished in the direction of the refreshment stand.

She turned to me. "My name is Lat. What's yours?"

I told her my name which she had great difficulty pronouncing. When she finally succeeded, she laughed at it. I have never since heard my name spoken so beautifully.

"Will you be long in Vietnam?" she asked.

"I don't think so," I answered. "With the curfew and the travel restrictions there isn't much to keep me here. I'd like to get out into the countryside; I'd like to meet the people, but there is no chance for that now."

"Yes, that is true. There are many restrictions. Some even we do not understand, but some are necessary. There is a war. But there are many things one can do in Saigon, even now."

She asked me many questions, as a child would, without regard for their personal nature. "What do you do in the United States? Why are you making this trip? Where did you get all the money necessary to travel so much? Are you very rich?"

I explained to her about my profession, told her of my

limited bank account and my reason for making the trip. She listened attentively, as if she would later be asked to repeat all she had heard. She accepted everything except the part about my limited resources.

"Americans are all very rich, I know. Sometimes they give me more in tips than my wages for the week. And you must have a great deal of money just to come so far. America is a very long distance from here. With the money for your passage, many Vietnamese could live very happily for a long time."

There was a moment of awkward silence. "I must go now," she said. "I have many things to show my group."

I wanted to see her again, but felt reticent, since I was unfamiliar with Vietnamese protocol. "Can you recommend a good restaurant for French food?" I asked clumsily.

"Yes, many."

"Would it be proper to ask you to dinner?"

"Do you want to ask me?"

"Yes."

"Then it is proper."

"Will you have dinner with me tonight?"

"Yes," she said simply. "Where is your hotel?"

"I'd be happy to pick you up," I said.

"I don't think so," she answered, matter-of-factly. "I'll meet you at your hotel."

I told her the name of the hotel and we agreed to meet at 8:30. "Au revoir," she said, and walked toward her group. I watched as, with great ease, she reassembled them, took the arm of a complaining woman and started off toward the gate.

I was ready by seven. As it was much too hot to wait in my room, I wandered down onto the hotel veranda. It was crowded with people, mostly military, having their aperitif. They were noisy and seemed carefree. On a raised platform at the foot of the garden, a small orchestra played French songs badly. I ordered a cold drink and sat at the only empty table. It was one of the first times I had worn a tie and coat for quite some time, and I felt hot, uncomfortable and conspicuous.

I was there only a few moments before an American couple approached me. "There doesn't seem to be any room, fella," the man drawled, "can me and the little lady join you for a drink?"

"Sure," I said, and stood up to introduce myself. They were Mr. and Mrs. Condon from Texas. They both ordered Scotch and soda, a most expensive drink in Asia. He drew out a large number of bills. "These piasters sure are a joke!" he said. "We just get used to one kind of money and it's time to start using another. The wife here is the bookkeeper."

"It's nothin'," she said, "you just divide by . . ." and she continued with a long explanation of how money was converted in each of the countries they had visited. They were on a six-week tour which had somehow qualified them as experts on Asia.

"Why most of the places are filthy holes, dirty as hell!" Mr. Condon said. "The people are all crooks and after only one thing—the American dollar. I hate the goddamn place, can't wait to get home. And that damn Calcutta. Did you ever see such a hole? Why the wife and I arrived and left the same day. Didn't even unpack our bags. Just got the hell out!"

"All those poor starving children," Mrs. Condon added sadly. "Why don't they do something? It's terrible! And the beggars! They're so dirty! Thank God for Western hotels! At least there you can have a shower and meet some civilized people."

"There wasn't one nice hotel in Calcutta," Mr. Condon said.

"Yes, there was, dear," his wife corrected him with finality, "our agent just couldn't book us there."

The conversation continued in this vein for some time.

Mrs. Condon: "The Taj Mahal was nice but they should spend their money on feeding some of those skinny children."

Mr. Condon: "What they need in these countries is some American know-how and get-up-and-go. I think the whole damn bunch are lazy, and it gripes my behind that they wait for us to give them handouts."

Mrs. Condon: "What's there to buy in Vietnam? I need a million souvenirs to take home. We have to get something for the kids, you know. We have six grandchildren. Show him the pictures, dear."

Mr. Condon: "And everything's so damned expensive here. You can't turn around without having one of those smelly Chinks with his hand out. Terrible!"

Mrs. Condon: "I think the people are awful. There are a few nice ones, I guess, but there isn't one of them who wouldn't profit from a good bath, a bottle of deodorant and a dentist's office."

I was relieved to see Lat walking up the stairs. I stood as she approached. She walked directly to the table. She was wearing the native dress, this time in deep blue. Her hair was loose and down over her back.

"This is Lat," I said, as I did not know her full name. "Mr. and Mrs. Condon." They greeted her pleasantly.

Mr. Condon offered her a drink which she accepted, seating herself at his side.

"You are from Texas," she laughed.

"That's right. How did you know?"

"Oh, I can always tell a man from Texas, he's so big and strong and talks so slow and nice."

I thought I saw Mrs. Condon squirm slightly in her seat.

"Are you from these parts?" she asked Lat.

"Yes, I am Vietnamese. I was born in Saigon." After a moment of silence, Lat spoke again. "Oh, Mrs. Condon, what a beautiful pin. Where did you get it?"

Mrs. Condon beamed, a bit more at ease, "Just a little something I picked up in Bangkok."

"It's lovely."

The conversation became more animated. Lat's presence made even the Condons more palatable. She laughed and listened attentively, from time to time glancing toward me as if she could sense my uneasiness.

"It's so nice to meet the people of the country," Mrs. Condon said. "We haven't had much of a chance. We've got six weeks, and though that's a lot of time, Asia's pretty big."

"Six weeks for all of Asia?" Lat asked. "On a tour?"

"No sirree," Mr. Condon answered, looking proudly at his wife. "We're on our own. No tour for us. All ya do is get herded around like cattle. No, the Mrs. and I decided we'd do it alone. Our travel agent arranges everything for us, of course, hotels, local tours, plane reservations, the works, but we're on our own. They meet us at the airport in each country, of course. We've never seen so damn many markets and temples and historic places in our lives."

"Shall we go, Lat?" I said.

"Oh, won't you have another drink," the Condons pleaded, as though dreading the thought of being faced with another evening alone together.

"We really haven't the time," I said.

"Well, it's sure been nice," Mr. Condon said.

"Yes," Mrs. Condon echoed. "See you again."

We left the veranda in silence. When we reached the street Lat turned to me. "I feel very sorry for them," she said. "Would you like to ask them to join us?"

"I think not," I said, a bit thankful to be away.

"Americans are like children," she said. "I like them very much. They make me feel like a very large mother, and I want to take care of them. The French are very independent. The Germans are forceful and know their own minds. The Italians are very relaxed and enthusiastic and don't much care. But the Americans always need someone!"

The restaurant of Lat's choice was comparable to most on the Champs Elysées in Paris. The decor was French, with the large menu in French and Vietnamese. All the waiters spoke English as well as French and Vietnamese.

The dinner was cooked to perfection and the wine tasted especially fine after so many months. When we were presented with the bill, Lat commented, "You see, you are a wealthy man!" I didn't explain that I could easily live for a week on the cost of this single meal but after several weeks of rice, dahl, chapate, gruel and sushi, it was well worth the expense.

"You would like our Vietnamese food," she said. "It's really very fine."

The night was beginning to cool and we walked down one of the main boulevards, brightly lit and busy with people taking their evening promenades. It was hardly imaginable that somewhere, not far off, a war was raging. Saigon was still "The Paris of the Orient." It was well planned and lovely with long, broad tree-lined streets, busy sidewalks swept clean and well-lit, superbly arranged shop windows. The traffic and crowds were as noisy as those of Paris and almost as plentiful.

"No one even seems aware there is fighting going on," I commented.

"Oh," Lat said, "we are aware. But what would you have us do? I am nineteen years old and I have never known anything but war. It has been going on in one form or another for over twenty-five years. One simply lives. In Saigon, except for the soldiers on leave, occasional bombs or fires and some grumbling, it's the same as ever."

She was silent for a long while. "It is very difficult under our present regime. It is very much disliked, especially by the Buddhists. I am a Catholic, a Christian, so it is easier for me, but for the Buddhists life is unbearable." She looked very seriously at me and continued. "I do not understand politics, but I wonder why your country continues to remain here. Have you seen the bombed palace? My people are trying to say how unhappy they are, but. . . ." her voice trailed off into silence.

"I guess our government thinks you'd prefer this to the Communists," I said.

She looked at me, incredulously. "Communism?" she asked, "for Buddhists and Christians? I think that all we really want is freedom, to eat, some peace. We are all tired of war. We are happy people. I want to dance again before I forget how. I will be an old lady before I can go to another party!" she laughed. "But we are being so serious. I'll take you to something very interesting, a Vietnamese opera."

The opera had already begun. The theater was packed and extremely noisy. The production, half-spoken, half-sung, was more like an operetta. The story was easy to follow, a variation on the usual horse opera in an exotic, royal setting. It had the inevitable villain dressed in black, the very pure heroine and hero in white, the confused parents and abused citizenry, and the corrupt go-between. Action was the most important element. The hero gouged out his eyes within full view of the audience. Blood and cries of anguish were the delights of the evening. Stabbing, torture

and brutal murders were all performed with carefully con-
trived special effects; the more real, gory and gruesome the
action, the more delighted and noisy grew the audience, as
if they were experiencing some special emotional release.
They cheered the hero, hissed the villain, and had a great
time.

It was very late when the opera ended. Much to my
surprise, Lat asked to be put into a taxi and would not allow
me to see her home. She thanked me, promised to call the
next day, and sped off into the crowded streets.

The next day I waited for Lat's call, never wandering
far from the hotel. I found excuses to wash the clothes which
had been accumulating in a plastic bag in my suitcase, to
write letters to people who surely must have given me up
for dead, and to lie about on my bed and watch the palms
on the veranda stand stately still in the heat of the day.

There was no call that day.

That evening I again met the Condons. We had a drink
together at their invitation. They had been most intrigued
by Lat.

"I only wish I were young and fancy free again," Mr.
Condon said.

Mrs. Condon giggled.

"We're going to see Saigon at night tonight. The tour is
picking us up at 9:00. 'Course, I don't know what there is
to see in Saigon that's worth twenty-five dollars, but at least
it's better than sitting around this dump!" Mr. Condon rum-
bled. "Thank God we leave in the morning. We're off to
Cambodia to see some damn place called Angkor Wat.
Know the place? Our agent told us we had to see it. What
is it, some damn temple?"

I tried my best to explain a bit about Angkor, never taking
my eyes off the desk for a possible call.

The night was hot and sultry. When the Condons left, I

took a short walk. The street noise seemed especially loud and irritating; the motor scooters, deafening. I was amazed that I had not really noticed them before. I was beginning to find Saigon oppressive.

I returned to the hotel to find a note from Lat. It read simply, "Work did not permit me any free time to see you again. Thank you for the nice evening. Continue to have a good trip. You are really very nice. Return to Saigon after the war. Lat."

A few days later, I left Vietnam.

chapter 7

Bali

In the Inn of the world there is room for everyone.
To turn your back on even one person, for what-
ever reason, is to run the risk of losing the central
piece of your jigsaw puzzle.

Ratal

I arrived in Bali on the day before Christmas. The bus driver, with a broad, betel nut-stained smile, stopped at a fork in the road. He pointed down a narrow paved street. Like most roads in Bali, it cut straight into the dense jungle, only to vanish in heat mist. "Ubud," he said.

I thanked him, shook his hand, waved goodbye to my fellow passengers, and waited as he started the small rickety bus with a loud blast and disappeared down the main road.

The morning was still relatively cool. December was a good month for Bali, with hot days, balmy nights and long afternoons ending in spectacular, multi-colored sunsets.

From what I had been told in Denpasar, the palace of the Agung was less than an hour's walk down the road. In Asia, distance is measured by time.

I took a firm grip on my suitcase and started out. Brown-skinned Balinese draped in gorgeous batik began to appear from nowhere, carrying bundles of fresh fruit, bottles of various colored liquids, animals in various stages of approaching death, and plump, smiling naked infants. The almond-shaped, bare-breasted young girls moved quickly like ballerinas, while handsome hard-bodied boys, whose skin glistened like deep waxed mahogany, ran and chattered together.

Occasional dirt paths cut their way into the jungle from the narrow road, suggesting the location of small settlements here and there in the brush. Small wooden shacks, partially hidden between bushes on the banks, towered precariously over the road. Crooked stone steps rose to doors which stood open, welcoming the cool early morning darkness.

Houses became more frequent, more people appeared, and soon I approached the center square of Ubud. There, towering over everything in pink beauty was the wall of the palace compound, facing what seemed to be a large open-air assembly area. On the opposite side of the road were several small shops selling wood carvings and the famous paintings of Bali.

The Agung had received a letter from one of his hundreds of relatives throughout the islands of Indonesia and was expecting me. He was a rather jolly, rotund man, dark-skinned, with a friendly smile whose favorite expression, learned while attending school in England, was rather shockingly, "Gee, goodness me!"

"Gee, goodness me," he greeted me. "I knew you were coming, but I did not know exactly when. Welcome."

Two little boys ran out and attached themselves to his fat legs below the drape of his knee-length sarong. "These are my sons," he said proudly, "and those playing there are also my children. And, gee, goodness me, those women on the veranda are my wives. You will meet them tonight. Tonight we talk."

There was a moment of silence as he detached his children gently from his legs and lifted them affectionately in his arms. "Ratab," he called. "Ratab is my best servant." Ratab appeared dressed in Western-style clothes, all in white. His face was round, dark, alive with dancing eyes, a broad smile, and even, white teeth. Ratab stood staring at me while the Agung continued, "Will you stay here on the palace grounds or will you take one of the cottages on the hill near the river?" He did not wait for my answer but continued, "I have many interesting guests now, an American school teacher on vacation from Sumatra, an Irish painter who came for a week and has been here for seven years, and a very important person from the Consulate in Djakarta. There is still room in the palace. There is no one in the cottages."

"I think I'd like a cottage, if it means no additional trouble."

"Gee, goodness me, no. Ratab will be there with you, to take care of what you may need. It will be good for him, too. It will give him a chance to practice his English. We will send a servant ahead to get the place ready, and Ratab will show you how to get there. It is not too far."

As we started out of the court he called, "Gee, goodness me, come to dinner at seven."

We reached the road and started up the slow incline which led to the cottages. Ratab explained that he was seventeen years old, had a secondary school education and was now studying English in Denpasar. He was neither shy nor aggressive, but had a simple honest quality which was most charming. "You will take the cottages," he said. "I'm happy that you chose to stay there. There are many flowers and birds, and all is green. You get no dust from the road, and at night, when all is quiet, you can hear the song of the river. I stay there only when we have a guest. I am happy that you chose the cottage."

"It's beautiful here," I said. "It's a perfect place to spend Christmas."

"Christmas?" he asked. "What is Christmas?" This was unexpected. I had forgotten that there were many in the world who had never heard of Christianity.

"Christmas is the birthday of the Christian God, Jesus."

Ratab was perhaps the most curious individual I met in all my travels. Not simply a child-like curiosity but a deep interest obsessed him which was not satisfied until he understood exactly, with no question, what was implied or stated. He would never allow a question in his mind to remain unanswered.

"Who is the Christian God, Jesus?" he asked.

"Like your God, Vishnu. Well, sort of."

So started a rather simple telling of the Christmas story. Until this time, as often as I had heard the story, I had never realized what an exciting, charming and delightfully mystical tale it was. As I spoke, we walked through a dense rain forest of lush ferns, tall tropical trees and shrubs which easily dwarfed us, and flowers which hung everywhere in splashes of orange, yellow, pink, red, all entwined in the deep green of the landscape.

"I hear the river!" I interrupted my tale.

"Yes," Ratab answered. "It flows beneath the rope bridge ahead. But why would not the people allow Mary and Joseph to share their bed?"

I explained that neither Mary nor Joseph knew anyone in Bethlehem. This did not seem to make any difference to Ratab who insisted that someone should have made room for them in their bed.

"But they did not know that Mary was to give birth to their God, Jesus."

"That is not important," Ratab insisted matter-of-factly. "If Mary was traveling, if she was going to have a child, what matter if it were God or not? They should have given her a place to rest." There was certainly no arguing with this statement and I realized that there were some things I would never be able to explain to Ratab. I changed the subject, telling him about the significance of the Christmas tree. He was delighted with the idea and the giving of gifts, and laughed at the thought of a "jolly old Santa Claus," though I was not quite able to explain the connection between Santa Claus and the God, Jesus, to his satisfaction. "Why does not Santa Claus dress as Jesus?" he asked.

In a few moments we had come to a steep gorge, green and rich with color. At the bottom rushed a clear river, purring its way over and around rocks of odd shapes and sizes.

"This is our river," Ratab said. "It is a most sacred river because all our ancestors are buried here and their remains flow in the stream. We bathe here each day. You must bathe with us."

We crossed over the shaky rope bridge. Below were groups of naked people, splashing happily in the river, washing their sarongs or drying their brown bodies in the warm sun.

"Tell me of the snow in Bethlehem," Ratab said suddenly. "Of what use is snow? And then you must explain why they would not let Mary and Joseph stay at the inn."

After crossing the bridge, we made a sharp turn to our right and down a steep stairway. There, in a natural garden of grass and flowers, stood four square, thatch-roofed cottages.

"You must take the top cottage," Ratab told me. "From it you can see the mountains, the river, the valley and the sky."

Each cottage had a large living area covered with palm branches and open to the jungle. The bedroom was half as large, with wall-length, pull-up shutters and a small West-ern-style bed. The bathroom had a cesspool and a stone sink into which fresh water was poured daily for washing. The water was carried up from the river. All about the rooms were small oil lamps made of clay. The hard dirt floor was swept clean.

It was now shortly after noon. The sun was hot, but pleasant. Ratab went off for a while to send the houseboy for food. The Christmas story had made a great impression on him. He accepted it without question except for the fact that Mary had been denied lodging. "Certainly, two persons do not take very much space. It is very strange, indeed."

I looked out into the afternoon. The sun's rays pierced through leaves and flowers livening each one with design and color.

When Ratab returned he was followed by a tall, thin young man with shy and downcast eyes. His brown body of drawn muscle and bone was partially covered with a fading batik loincloth. His long legs were straight and muscular. He carried a tray covered with small dishes of exotic foods, which he set before me. Then, he left without a word.

Ratab sat beside me and explained each dish as I ate the subtle tasting, savory mixtures. Now and again one could hear the sound of footsteps and laughter as the natives walked down the cliff on their way to the river. Some paused to look at us, seemingly delighted that one of the cottages was again occupied.

When I finished eating, Ratab said, "Now you must rest. Later, I will take you to bathe. If you want anything, call Adja. He will be here with you all the time, night and day." He had no sooner said this when Adja appeared to remove the tray he had brought. He did not raise his eyes as we were introduced.

I stripped and climbed into the bed. From a reclining position I could see the tops of the tall palms, some orange and purple bougainvillea, the fluffy edge of a very white cloud, and the blue sky. As the heat became more intense, the afternoon awakened all at once with the myriad sounds of life in Bali: the buzz of the insects, the murmur and splash of the river, soft footsteps, voices, and laughter. Adja entered silently and lowered the shutters. I fell asleep instantly.

It was late afternoon when Ratab awakened me. It was still hot and my sheets were wet with perspiration. "It is time to bathe," he said. He carried a patterned batik which he helped me tie around my body.

The path down along the cliff to the river was only wide enough for one person to move along, with caution. It was patted firm by the many hard-soled bare feet that mounted and descended each day. Ferns and flowers bordered it, hanging gently just out of reach.

What before had been the constant sibilant sound of the river became a roar as we descended into the gorge. From above, the river had seemed narrow and gracefully bouncy, but at close view it revealed its rushing strength. In some places the water was clear enough for us to discern the stone bottom; in others the river floor vanished in foam and deep color. Clever damming created the bathing areas. A group of men in various bathing postures, tanned and hardened by the sun and streaked with soap foam, greeted us as we reached the river. Ratab pointed to the clear spot on a large rock. "Here," he said. We stripped and under the curious eyes of the other bathers plunged into the cold water. The initial shock brought the usual reaction, causing the others to laugh, relax, and resume what they were doing before our arrival.

When we had soaped and bathed and were lying in the

sun to dry, the group assembled about Ratab with expressions that seemed to ask, "Well, who is this strange white man?" Ratab explained with understandable gestures that I was staying in the cottage on the hill as the guest of the Agung, and that I was from far-off America. One by one they glanced sideways at me, my smile meeting theirs in a language of its own.

Through Ratab we all learned a few simple facts about each other: I was a professor from America, one was a painter, another made wood carvings, others worked their fathers' rice fields, and so on. As our initial strangeness wore off, we each found our own language to tell our story.

"House." "Your." "There."

"Water." "Cold." "Nice."

"This rock better, smoother."

"Sun warmer here."

"Come, lie with us here."

Soon I was surrounded by naked, shining bodies, by lips murmuring in a strange wondrous language, and by smiles rivaling each other for warmth and beauty.

Calmly Ratab began to talk. He was obviously telling them something which meant a great deal to him. The group was intent on every word. I found myself listening along with the others. Every now and then I seemed to hear, "Jesus," "Mary," "Bethlehem," and it became clear that he was telling them the Christmas story. I lay back and closed my eyes, lulled by the sounds of the lilting language.

We all left the river together, walking up the path directly toward the setting sun. As it dropped into the trees, it seemed to cling to a group of drooping palm leaves, then reluctantly release them and dip out of sight behind the rain forest, leaving the sky a hundred colors. I said goodbye to the group at my cottage door and stood listening to their laughter and watching them as they scaled the last small incline and vanished into the sunset. Ratab said he would return in a few hours to escort me to the palace for dinner.

As I dressed that evening I seemed to hear a soft moan, or was it a strange weeping? I walked out into the dusk. The cry seemed to be coming from the dense rain forest across the river where there was certainly no human habitation. At first I felt sure that it must be the breeze which had suddenly come up, but then it sounded too human, too desperate. Night came suddenly with a deep purpleness which covered everything. I only then realized that the oil lamps in the cottage were lit. I had neither seen nor heard Adja though obviously he was very much present. Entering the bedroom I found him lighting another small lamp.

The weeping sound seemed even louder now. I took Adja by the arm and pointed toward the sound in the blackness. He did not immediately understand, but after a moment he nodded. Then, for the first time he spoke. His voice was at once excited and animated. Of course, I understood nothing. Upon finishing his complicated explanation, which he assumed I understood, he took me into the bathroom and showed me the clear water he had carried from the river for my shave.

Shortly Ratab arrived, dressed in a richly-colored sarong. His dark hair was partly hidden under a small two-cornered hat of red silk. His chest was bare, broad and smooth. He carried a small oil lamp to light our way to the palace. We crossed the footbridge in silence. The night noises were overpowering. The river's voice sounded clear and constant although the river could not be seen. I wondered about the moan which was no longer audible, but I did not want to disturb the night mood with my questions.

The Agung was silhouetted in the palace entrance when we arrived. He seemed younger.

"Gee, goodness me," he said. "You have come at last.

It is the birthday of my youngest son. They are waiting for us." He took my arm and led me through the small dimly lit square and into a cluster of trees and flowers.

"Ratab told me that you related the Christmas story to him. Yes, it will be Christmas. I have ordered a Christmas dinner for you. You seem to have won over the young men of the village. You will find them very sincere and very good. I am happy that you want to know them."

We entered another court, typical of the inner courtyards in Balinese homes, surrounded by tall walls and containing several small structures—huts, a place of worship, and studios. In the rear of the compound was a small elevated stage. Informally seated about it were all of the Agung's children, twenty or more, and several beautiful women. On the platform were an old priest, a woman and the birthday child.

The Agung mounted the platform, kissed the child, and sat on a large chair. He insisted that I follow him and sit next to him in a place of honor. The ceremony was short and consisted mostly of sharing an odd-tasting drink and murmuring a short prayer. This was followed by much rejoicing on the part of the children and by the eating of wondrous sweets and savory fruits.

A large white sheet was then stretched across the platform and after everyone had gathered before it, a puppeteer worked behind it treating us to a fantastic shadow play. The story was simple and required only a word or two of explanation. The Agung was delighted that I was acquainted with the Ramayana, as it was an episode of this epic which was being produced. For about fifteen minutes Rama battled the forces of evil with those of good, and the children watched entranced as he succeeded. The puppeteer supplied all the voices and manipulated the various graceful, grotesque puppets with ease.

The Agung rose when the performance was over. "You must see the truly great stories done by the master." He smiled to the assembled group. A child ran to the Agung to be picked up and hugged to his bare shoulder. "Gee, goodness me," he said, handing the child to one of the women. "Let us go to dinner."

We walked back to the palace dining room, which was lit with oil lamps of great beauty. There, on a large round table were more than twenty dishes with a large, crackly suckling pig in the center. The odors were fantastic. Seated on cushions around the table were the other guests. The American school teacher was about thirty years old and wore Balinese dress. He was obviously trying hard to appear Indonesian. The Irish painter had a long, straggly beard, spoke with a brogue and smiled deeply and calmly as if he had achieved some secret insight from his seven years in Bali. Only the Indonesian dignitary from the Consulate was in Western-style clothing and seemed strangely out of place in the group.

When the introductions were over I was seated on a pillow at the table and two graceful women silently began to serve us. The Agung cut the pig, taking great pains to see that each of us had his share of the crackling skin. Each dish was elegant: fish, vegetables, rice, fowl, fruit.

After the dinner, the group relaxed on their pillows and the conversation started. The Agung's participation revealed his facility with the English language, his keen wit, his clear mind and his exciting ideas about life.

"Here in Bali things have not changed as in other parts of Indonesia. Somehow we continue to live as we please. It is true there is some hunger and poverty, but this is not a new condition among our people. We have learned to live with nature. We are a people who love happiness. We need little: we dance, we play our music, we work. Art comes easily in Bali, for all is art, and the search for beauty is not difficult. It is everywhere. Beauty is our way of life. If you say, 'growl not, stomach, there is nothing to put in thee,' long enough, the stomach learns and growls less. In Ubud we are better off than most, for we are a colony of artists. My people are painters and dancers and wood carvers. Tourists come to look. We show them our beauty. We have changed our painting in some cases to suit their taste. Therefore we have to some small extent compromised with the rest of the world. But compromise enables us to eat, sleep and live as we please. We are a superstitious people. We are affectionate without being passionate. We are strong without forgetting how to be dependent. We are proud without losing sight of the strength in being humble. I hope," he said to me, "that you will stay long enough to know us."

The evening passed too quickly. Ratab came out of the nowhere into which he had disappeared carrying another oil lamp.

"Ah, how quickly time passes. It is time for us to go already," the Agung said as he rose and rubbed his round belly. "Merry Christmas to you all, and to all a good night."

"Is that not Charles Dickens?" he laughed.

The night had become lighter. The sky was filled with stars. We returned to the cottage in silence. Ratab put his arm warmly about my shoulders and held the lamp before us. "It is a beautiful Christmas night," he said. When we reached the incline, Ratab preceded me down the side and helped me toward the cottage. In the doorway stood a banana tree which had been trimmed into the shape of a pine tree. On each branch were tied several flowers of assorted colors and scattered about the tree were small clay oil lamps like tiny stars. "Your Christmas tree," he said simply.

I stood in the darkness before the tree. The lamp lights flickered slightly in the warm breeze. My eyes welled with tears. Ratab watched me closely. Assuming this was the tradition he mustered tears and joined me in a good cry. After some time we entered the cottage. The room was crowded with some of the same boys I had bathed with and others I had not seen before. Each, Ratab indicated, had brought me a Christmas present, bananas, coconuts, papayas, pieces of batik, paintings and even oil lamps of various shapes and sizes.

I sat on the floor among them, and the conversation never stopped. They all wanted to hear the story of Christmas from me. With Ratab translating, no more flowery presentation was ever made. When the story was told, I passed the fruit and, while they were eating, went into the bedroom. What did I have to give *them*? I had so little with me. I took everything that I could give away from the suitcase, my T-shirts, briefs, shirts, socks, no matter what—it was the spirit. They were all delighted with their gifts and discarded their elaborate batiks to put on jockey shorts and T-shirts, all too large for their slim bodies. They began to dance and sing and were pleased when I joined them.

In the midst of all the laughter the sounds from across the river could again be heard. This time I felt sure the sound was a human weeping.

"What is that, Ratab?" I asked.

"Oh, it is the spirits," he said simply. "Bali has many spirits. The forest is full of them. They are everywhere. The spirit you hear is a very sad one. They say that he was Dutch and that he loved a girl from Ubud and was killed in the war. The girl leaped from this very cliff into the sacred river, so she too has never died. Do not have fear. Spirits who love, do no harm. Bali is a land of spirits."

The festivity continued for a while and then Ratab announced that I must be tired and that it was time for sleep.

Then he explained that several of the guests had asked for the honor of staying overnight.

"When you have made a new friend," he explained, "it is bad manners to leave him." The bed was small but Ratab picked six of the guests to join me. They put me in the middle and arranged their bodies about me. Like joyfully exhausted children they fell asleep instantly: one holding my hand, another with his head on my shoulder, another with his leg over mine.

I stared up at the thatched roof and listened to the even breathing of my bed partners. The light of a single oil lamp danced about the room. Outside the Christmas tree glittered beneath the stars.

Ratab, who had taken the place of honor at my side, slid his arm under my head. "I still don't understand why they could not make room for Mary."

After a moment of silence he said, "Well, Merry Christmas," and fell asleep.

chapter 8

Ceylon

Happiness, for us, has its own measure, though beauty and riches can often tip the scale.

Mano

The buses streamed in until the large square overlooking the lake in Kandy was completely congested. Dark, dhoti-clad worshippers, some with painted faces, walked toward the Temple of the Tooth. Gaily colored elephants in festive regalia swayed clumsily along the shore of the lake. Chants were already arising from the large temple where thousands of worshippers had come to prostrate themselves before the Sacred Tooth of the Great Buddha.

The large hall just outside the ornately decorated sanctum sanctorum where the Tooth was housed was completely filled with bare-chested, sweaty bodies; kneeling, sitting, lying, standing in wait.

Flowers were everywhere and each worshipper carried at least a handful of brightly colored flower petals. Many had leis strung around their necks and wrists and blossoms between their toes.

The women in the group wore their best saris, often of

brightly colored silk which glistened in the light with in-definable color, like a magician's handkerchief which changes to red, blue, green, before your eyes.

Noise and activity dominated the scene: the unintelligible instructions shouted over blaring microphones to the obliv-ious mass, the chants of the worshippers, the shouts of the members of the press, and the screams of young boys scram-bling through the crowds or over the temple walls like small, agile lizards.

Saffron-robed priests, unmoved by the rising excitement, proceeded toward the temple gates at an even gait, each chanting and praying as if he were alone in the vast square.

The intoxicating odors of burning woods and incense together with their light smoke added a misty haze which gave the scene the aura of pre-dawn light.

The ceremony continued throughout the day. People pushed impatiently in every direction through the assembled worshippers, in long lines forming snake-like patterns of bodies in the crowd. Each person was finally admitted into the holy room in noisy procession. As each entered he threw his petals on the golden altar, hesitated a moment for prayer, and was impatiently pushed out by those behind him. There was time for a quick look at the Holy Relic on its tray of gold, then in an instant one was out of the temple, down the stairs, and back among the thousands still waiting in the square.

By dusk everyone had seen and prayed before the Sacred Tooth of Buddha, and all crowded back on their buses which moved slowly as they had come, back over the jungle road to Colombo or another village along the way.

By moonrise, the tiny city by the lake was again sub-merged in the stillness of the surrounding mountainous jun-gle, the moon shadows and the warm breeze.

That had been my first day in Kandy. I had arrived by

train the day before expressly for the ceremony. I met Mano on the ramp in Colombo, perhaps the most handsome boy I had seen in Asia: features dark and perfect, a combination of well-shaped lips, heavy black brows and hair, and large, almond eyes set apart by a sensitive nose. His skin was a light, smooth chocolate brown with a dash of color over his cheeks. His body was slim, strong and agile. He spoke clearly and distinctly.

"How do you find my country?" he asked me in lieu of formal introduction.

"I really don't know yet," I answered. "I've been here only a few days and I understand one can't judge Ceylon by Colombo."

"Oh, I agree," he smiled. "Wait until you see Kandy, I am sure you will find it enchanting. I was born there. My name is Mano Sahayam. Are you going to the Ceremony of the Tooth?"

"Yes."

"I, too, am going. These are our holidays from school."

"Are you at the University?"

"Yes, in law. That is the field my parents have chosen for me. I have no interest in law."

The train pulled up to the platform.

"Do you have a third-class ticket?" he asked.

"No, mine is for second."

"Well," he said, "they will allow you to sit in third class with a second-class ticket. Come with me." He took my suitcase and we boarded a large car, clearly marked "Third Class." To my surprise, it was the newest and most well-equipped of the train's cars. The seats were soft and luxurious and situated so that one could get the maximum view through large, tinted windows.

"This is the most beautiful third-class car I have seen in my travels," I commented. "Are they all like this?"

He laughed, "Indeed, no. Look at first class over there. It is terrible—old, worn, and ready to crumble. This car is a gift from the People's Republic of China to the people of Ceylon. It is one of many given expressly for our workers who must otherwise ride in third-class filth." He waited for my expression and reaction.

"A very clever bit of propaganda, indeed," he said for me. "The Americans have given us a great deal more, but I don't think the people who ride these trains have ever seen a thing from you which they could really understand. American aid has become a joke in Ceylon. You built a gigantic dam which has been abandoned dry. I forget how many thousands of dollars it cost. You assume that our needs are like yours, a rather silly assumption."

"I hope," Mano added suddenly, "that I do not offend you, speaking this way. The Americans I have met always speak freely."

I smiled.

He was pleased and continued to talk.

"We have come a long way in Ceylon, but we must go our own way. I don't believe we are ready for democracy in the American sense, at least not as I understand it. The British governed us like infants and left us as children. We are now seeking to find who we are. We are not sure who we are or where we want to be. When we find out, then we can make a choice. My father is a conservative. I am, perhaps, more of a socialist."

Thanks to Mano, the train trip was informative and delightful. As we neared Kandy he asked, "Where will you stay? You are a professor and can stay at the University. It is vacation time and there is much room. The food is terrible, but you can come to my home for meals."

There was a small university station before the train arrived in Kandy. We left the train there and walked a short distance to the campus. It was simple for Mano to arrange a room for me in one of the large dormitories, mostly vacant due to the recess.

Mano left me in the hands of several students who seemed more than eager to assume the responsibility and left for home on a borrowed scooter.

Life at the University was like that on any campus during the vacation period: quiet, deserted, with few students who appeared only for meals. Food was served family-style at communal tables—a few simple curry dishes accompanying mountains of steamed rice.

About sundown, Mano arrived with his usual smile. "I have my father's car. You are cordially invited to dinner."

It had rained that afternoon and everything shone, washed and fresh. The lake and the rain forest in the distance reflected the hues of the multi-colored sunset as we drove up the hill leading to Mano's house.

"The main part of the city is there," Mano pointed. "All roads lead to the temple. There, beyond the residential section, the jungle begins. There, you'll find the elephant baths. Have you been on an elephant yet?"

Mano's father was very sophisticated, handsome like his son, and spoke clipped British English. His mother and two sisters, all wearing saris, resembled each other with large eyes, deep olive skin and soft smiles.

"We are very happy to have you here," the father said, "my son told us about you. I, too, am an educator. I run a private school for several hundred children. Our home is part of the school which extends back for several meters. It is a pity that school is not in session or you could visit. We are on the British system, of course, and..." he continued.

Dinner was served. The food was hotly seasoned, but varied and delicious. The conversation at dinner mostly concerned Mano, and the problems he posed for the family. The parents felt that it was time for him to marry and settle down to raise a family. They had already chosen the girl, whom I was to meet later. She was from a good family, was highly educated, and had a fine dowry. Mano was objecting, they said, though all during dinner he said not a word.

When the meal was over we moved into the living room for coffee and shortly Mano's bride-to-be arrived with her parents. She was a very young girl, not over thirteen. Her body was small and shapeless within her neatly folded sari.

Mano did not say ten words the entire evening, nor did he once look at his chosen bride. Later, in the car, he said anxiously, "We are not living in the days when people could be bought and sold. I will not marry that tiny nothing!"

We drove in silence for some time. Finally he added, "I love someone else."

We stopped in front of a two-story white structure with a long stairway rising across the front to a second level.

"Come," he said.

We climbed the stairs to a large porch where Mano let himself into the house without even a knock. There were four attractive young people in the room, three girls and a boy, who all greeted Mano enthusiastically.

"We heard you were home."

"When did you return?"

"How long will you stay?"

Mano answered their questions briefly, then introduced me to the group. They all spoke excellent English.

One of the girls, fairer and taller than the others, wore a bright, orange sari. Her hair fell in a long dark braid over her back. Her manner was carefree and her smile warm and pleasant. Her name was Silva. It was instantly apparent that she was Mano's girl.

Within minutes the young people were engaged in animated conversation which led to dancing to precious records by Elvis Presley. They were enraptured by his garbled speech which they asked me to translate.

Several hours later, Mano drove me back to the University. He spoke eagerly of Silva. "She's an Indian, not Ceylonese. She works as a receptionist at our best hotel in Kandy. Her family lives in Colombo."

"Indians," he continued, "are looked down upon in Ceylon as an inferior race, without education or sophistication. They are mostly servants. My family would not speak to anyone of Silva's class and would certainly never consent to our marriage." He fell silent like any hapless lover.

I saw Mano with Silva often. They were delightful together. Their relationship was never discussed. They were always relaxed and full of fun. Together we took trips to the lush highlands and tea plantations of Nuwara Eliya, to Pulanerua and to Anuradhapura, where we sat under the ancient banyan tree beneath which Buddah had contemplated.

During these trips I met some delightful people. One was a young waiter who took great pride in showing me his daily gift to the Great Buddha. Each day he offered a small glass of precious Coca Cola, placing it with great care before the special altar decorated with sacred pictures, tiny candles and flowers in the tiny closet-like room he called his own. Another was a baker who worked in primitive splendor before a giant fire-lit oven making bread fit for the best tables in Europe; yet another was an American Peace Corps volunteer with a severely infected leg he did not wish to report because it might take him away from his work in a tiny rural school.

Silva enchanted everyone she met. She was vivacious,

charming, intelligent and helpful. She was, indeed, as precious as Mano considered her.

One afternoon, when we were alone, she confided, "Mano
is a very unhappy boy—spoiled, too. Nice, of course, and
pretty, but spoiled. He wants to marry against his parents'
wishes, you know, but he fears being disinherited. His family sees me as unworthy. They are trying to preserve a
custom which is fast vanishing from Ceylon. Mano knows
this, but he is weak. He wants me, but not enough. He will
marry the little one, you will see."

On the day before I was to leave Kandy, we went to the
elephant bath. The road leading to the bath was partly paved,
winding through the jungle for about three miles. Here, near
a large muddy bank, stood several elephants. Some were
stomach-high in the stream, others considering whether to
brave the stream's rush, while others, prodded about by
boys with huge sticks, moved slowly along the bank. Each,
in his turn, was urged roughly into the stream until he had
his fill.

We returned part way to Kandy by elephant. I wore only
walking shorts affording no protection between my legs and
the elephant except his coarse, hairy, moist, rough, hot skin.
He slid about under me like a large mold of warm jello: a
uniquely unpleasant experience.

Regretfully I left Mano, his family and Silva to their
common dilemma and returning to Colombo moved into the
Y.M.B.A. (Youth Men's Buddhist Association) in the center of the city. From my window I could see the busy harbor.
Several times each day the silence was broken by the sound
of jets roaring into the airport several miles away. It was
rather a jolt, for during my few weeks in Ceylon, I had
viewed the most primitive and the most modern—from
primitive medicine man to modern jet age technology—
within a very small area.

Mano drove to Kandy for my departure. Before I left he said bravely, "I shall marry Silva and you will be our best man."

I was touched. I thought of the enormous changes taking place in his country, changes in attitudes, feelings and visions of the future. Perhaps with time, I thought, even the fulfillment of Mano's wish was possible.

chapter 9

Southern
India

Pride and impatience in people may not be virtues, but sometimes there is a certain beauty in both.

Professor Gupta

Those who have known only the India of the north have not known India. One must wander the streets of Tiruchirappalli, watch the sun rise and set over the sea at Cape Comorin, experience a Madras bazaar, talk with student groups in Trivandrum, stroll the beautiful esplanade of Ernakulum, paddle the canals of Cochin or spend some time in the giant temple of Madura. Then go north and you may get a feel for this great subcontinent." His eyes sparkled with pride. Although his words sounded like those of a travel folder, I could not help feeling his enthusiasm and deep concern for my well-being.

When my plane from Ceylon landed in Tiruchirappalli, I was the only tourist in the group. During the confusion of customs inspection, I was given some advice by a young man, Mr. Matriam, a Southern Indian. "There are many things about staying in India," he told me, "that you should be prepared for before you set out alone. In the first place, it is like no other country in the world. The way of life is different, the philosophy is unique, the food and clothing, even your accommodations will be a new experience. Prepare yourself."

"Station rest houses are comfortable and convenient," he continued. "They are very inexpensive, too. Trains are the best means of transportation, though buses are fine."

We went together by bus as far as the train station where he left me, explaining that he was continuing to Madras on a later train.

The station faced the square and was surrounded by shops and small offices. The building had two levels with the train platform, luggage and mail rooms below while several small guest rooms, a restaurant and the hostel office were located on the level above. The woman in charge of rooms seemed quite impatient and abrupt. I later learned that this was merely the voice quality and manner of the Indian. She briefly surveyed her reservation list and said, "I have a double room. You must be prepared to share it, if you plan to stay longer than two days."

The room was narrow and very long with windows at each end. The rear windows overlooked the train tracks and those at the front looked onto the square. It was a clean room. The beds had sheets and were covered by neatly patched mosquito netting. Not far from the room, on a small porch, were a toilet and shower. In all, it was as I had been told; not luxurious, very clean, pleasant and certainly not expensive.

The city, Tiruchirappalli, is referred to, even by some Indians, as the "cesspool." It owes its infamy to over-population, dirty streets, lack of water, unbearable heat, poor sanitation and the prevalence of disease. I was prepared for the worst when I left my room and walked toward the central part of town.

By evening, I had strolled the length and breadth of the city. It was true that the roads were mostly unpaved and dusty, that the heat was intense, that people and animals defecated in the streets, that everything was dry, that odors were pungent and rank and that insects were everywhere. But there was also a contagious excitement that permeated the atmosphere and tempted me to look beyond such depressing externals.

The center of the city, before the temple, was the focus of excitement. Here, one could find everything at any time of the day or night. The temple entrance was through a high red and white wall. Men were dressed in the Indian dhoti, a white cloth wrapped loosely around the body and tied at the waist. Feet and trunks were bare, bodies strong and black. The women wore saris of orange, red, green, purple, white, some of dull, faded cotton showing many washings in muddy river water. Others wore crisp silk that swished and crackled with each movement. Fingers, toes and arms were covered with rings, ringlets, bracelets, armlets, anklets; all jingled and jangled with every movement.

The children were mostly naked and ran freely through the crowds, joyful and unafraid. Animals were everywhere—sacred cows, decorated red, white, green; elephants with faces painted like happy clowns; goats; chickens; frisky, mischievous monkeys; and stately, disinterested bulls. As at a flower festival, men had leis about their necks and women wore them in their hair. Like animated centerpieces, vendors were seated in their stands surrounded by fresh fruit. They wore blossoms in their heavily greased dark hair and between each toe. Long garlands of blooms hung in batches like rainbows at the temple entrance.

The temple itself rose like a medieval fort, visible from every point within the city and from far off into the vast deserts which surrounded it. It was carved from and built into a massive rock, hollowed into levels joined by a single, steep stairway through the center. Each floor had its cool room of stone: one dominated by a huge carving of the dancing, multi-armed Krishna with a wise, smiling face; another by the God-elephant holding a nude female figure on his knee; a third by Krishna again, depicted this time as a voluptuous woman with firm breasts and shapely body. Above this level there was still another room crowded with noisy worshippers where a group of musicians sat cross-legged on a stone altar, playing beautiful but strangely dissonant music.

There were several smaller chambers, too, all filled with people reciting repetitive incantations or chanting prayers before a caged phallus or carved statue.

There was little inhibition, abstraction or refinement in the style of worship. It was personal and human, each man busily seeking salvation in his own way, through one of the innumerable sects, cults and philosophies which comprise modern Hinduism. They prayed or performed the necessary exercises loudly, with passion and a childlike trust in what they were doing. Their religious path, as their God, was comprehensible to them: full of human frailty, some humor, and inevitable pain and desire. After all, was not Vishnu often found as a man? And certainly Shiva, the God of demons, was never reluctant to enjoy human favors.

The activities of the temple seemed to me like India herself: individual, real, beautiful, sensual, colorful and mystical. The Indian learned early from his scriptures that life would pass and that life's only reality was the illusion that it existed. It was his role to accept life as illusion, to lose himself as simply as a man among men. Everywhere there was evidence of the vitality of this belief.

My head was spinning with the color and confusion and wonder of Tiruchi. When I returned to the hostel that evening I found a note, very formally written, from a Professor Gupta who was interested in making my acquaintance.

After dinner, I followed his written directions, given so precisely, to a small college on the outskirts of the city. I asked for Professor Gupta. After some time an extremely overweight, very dark, middle-aged man appeared. He was dressed with a Western-style coat and tie even in the evening's oppressive heat. "I am Professor Gupta," he said, extending a pudgy hand. As I took it I felt rings on all but two fingers and a palm clammy and wet with perspiration. "I was told of your arrival by Mr. Matriam, the young gentleman you met at the airport." He spoke formally, in an American style of speech rather than the usual English of his countrymen with its British accent.

He ushered me into his small office, turned on the overhead fan and motioned for me to be seated. Dropping his large frame into his desk chair with rather a thump he added, "I'm a professor here but my home is in Madras. I was educated in America, of course, as you can tell from my accent. I'm always interested in any Americans who come through Tiruchi. They are so very few." He spoke as if he were reciting a memorized speech.

He patted his forehead gently with a large white handkerchief, folded it neatly and replaced it in his pocket with much effort. "It's damn hot this evening! This place can be deadly. Only insects thrive on the conveniences of this city. A cesspool! Would you like a short walk?"

"Yes, very much." I was not sure I liked Mr. Gupta. He seemed distant, formal, cold. After all, he had requested the meeting; yet he seemed almost annoyed by having to entertain me, as if I were an added inconvenience. Each movement pained him in some way.

It was not much cooler outside than in his office. The streets of Tiruchi were now brightly lit, still crowded and noisier than ever. It was obviously time for food. For a few rupees one could buy rice and curry or some delectable candy made from coconut and honey and wrapped neatly in leaves, ground ices sweetened and made colorful with artificial flavors, freshly squeezed juice of sugar cane, or, of course, betel nuts.

Mr. Gupta saw all these things as additional personal annoyances: the cane squeezer crowded the sidewalk, the cooked coconut smelled rancid, the sight of the curry made him ill and the ground ices were surely lethal.

"My major field is American literature. I am something of an expert on Whitman, Emerson, Melville and Thoreau. Of course, I know the minor authors such as Hemingway and Steinbeck, but I feel that modern American literature has not had a single important person since Twain, don't you agree?" He never afforded me an opportunity to answer. "Just people who satisfy themselves with badly written, best-selling trash about perverted sex," he grumbled as he plodded along the dusty road. "I suppose you find Tiruchi rather disgusting?" he added.

"Not at all," I assured him, "I find it exciting. Fascinating. I've never seen anything like it. A bit mystifying."

"Like a strange animal in a zoo?"

His remark caught me off guard. "I like it here," I said at last, not trying to hide my annoyance. "I came here because I wanted to experience India."

"Frankly, I can't understand anyone coming here of his own free will. I find this city depressing." He reached for his handkerchief but did not use it. Instead, he nervously replaced it in his pocket.

"I spent the day in the temple," I told him, changing the subject. "I don't know when I've seen such feeling for life. So much color and joy. I don't find the city depressing at all."

"The heat is depressing, the dirt is depressing, the people are depressing. I can't speak for the temple as I've never been in it myself." He said this so condescendingly that had he not been serious I would have thought that he was trying to be amusing, like a cynical character from an Oscar Wilde play.

"I could understand someone visiting Madras, Mysore, Bangalore, perhaps even Cochin if the weather were favorable, but what can one possibly find here? I can only suspect that you came to be amused by staring at the natives."

Suddenly he stopped, sighed deeply and said, "I'm parched; I must have a cup of tea. I know a place where we might risk a cup of tea. Tea is boiled, you know—clean. My dear Doctor, I fear you must learn to forgive these primitive conditions if you plan to spend any length of time in Southern India."

We entered the tea shop and sat at a small wooden table. The waiter, a thin, dark boy, came immediately.

"Cha," Mr. Gupta pronounced distinctly, adding several specific instructions which I was unable to understand. His tone was disdainful, firm. "You must instruct these people precisely. So stupid, you know."

He stared at his hands, fingering his rings with pudgy fingers as he spoke. "So, my dear Doctor, you are planning an extensive trip through mysterious India. Well, I hope you find what you are seeking. And I am still wondering what that might be."

"Well," I started, but he did not allow me to finish.

"The temple at Madura. That is really quite lovely, but now the fools are painting the damn thing like a Christmas tree. Finally it will look like nothing less than a giant pyramid of circus characters. Pearls to swine!" he said, "Pearls to swine! Madras is lovely, but the sea makes any place bearable, isn't that right?" The tea came. The waiter placed it before us cautiously and left.

"Well at least they make a decent cup of tea here," he sighed.

When I left Gupta that evening, I was angry and did not care ever to see him again, so I was surprised when he invited me to join him the next morning on a trip to visit the Temple of the Bull in Tanjore.

"I shall try to get a car," he said, "but we may be required to take the blasted bus." He did not wait for my reply, but forced a smile, extended his sweaty, fat hand and said in his best American manner, "So long! See you tomorrow," and, with great effort, plodded off down the dirt road toward the college, mopping his forehead continuously and grumbling.

I hoped he would not come in the morning. I tried to think of several excuses not to go but when he arrived, sweating and puffing, it was impossible to reject him. He was very apologetic for being unable to get a car. "We shall have to take that damn bus," he said.

Actually the bus was rather pleasant. It was overcrowded but we had seats and with the warm air blowing on our faces through open windows, it was not too uncomfortable. I was relieved to find Gupta not as talkative as he had been during our previous meeting, which afforded me the pleasure of watching rural Indian life without caustic comment.

We passed mile after mile of parched earth, where not even a weed seemed to grow. Animals whose skin sagged over sharp bones and whose frothy mouths attested to their need for food and water stood like statues before dry water holes. Nearly naked farmers worked with crude implements on small patches of green. The sky was sparkling clear, cloudless. The sun beat down fiercely, as if magnified, determined to scorch man and his earth.

In contrast to this, even Tanjore's bareness seemed an oasis with its small cluster of brave structures washed white by the sun, standing as shady shelters against the heat.

The temple was closed. "What nonsense," Markham fussed, "we'll have it opened at once." He waddled over to the caretaker's house and, with much gesture and vocalization, obtained permission for us to enter. The caretaker made it clear, however, that we could not enter in Western clothes.

"Stupid, childish nonsense!" Gupta shouted, but on this point the man was adamant. Gupta led me to a small store where we could purchase dhotis, mumbling all the way. "Stupid! Stupid! Stupid! I have not worn one of these things in years. I feel damn ridiculous!" he complained, tying it around his fat hairy belly. "Stupid superstitions! When will we grow up?"

Within the temple on a high pedestal rested the giant bronze bull.

"You probably know that the bull was the animal chosen to carry the God Shiva to earth. So you will find him honored all over India. A sacred bull, indeed!"

Gupta conceded that the bronzed animal was impressive in its appearance of strength and expression of gentle, refined wisdom. "You wouldn't expect to find such subtlety of craftsmanship on a bull, would you?" he said, studying it closely as if seeing it for the first time. "Yes, I thought you should see this. It is quite lovely."

Gupta continued to confuse me. His attitude toward his country and its people was less than tolerant, kind and accepting. His attacks were vicious, yet he seemed very concerned that I enjoy and see carefully the very things he attacked. Although he showed no pleasure in his self-appointed position as my personal guide, he continued to insist on showing me as much as possible. It was as if he were almost afraid to allow me to miss something or perceive without guidance.

He consented, after several invitations, to have dinner with me one evening. He arrived mopping his forehead as usual. Each time we met he seemed a bit more relaxed. Now, he even smiled occasionally.

"Good evening, my dear Doctor," he said. "I'm famished!"

As we dined in Tiruchi's best restaurant, Mr. Gupta proved that there was good reason for his rotund shape. He requested second helpings of almost everything. "The food here is quite good. Our college food is atrocious! But that's true in the States, too. Fit only for the empty-headed youths it sustains. I, for one, love to eat. I always think it is such a pity that those of us who do have a passion for food and no vanity about the results cannot live in a place like Italy or Paris where food is respected and cooking is an art. Give me a good stuffed goose, fresh trout almondine, vegetables with hollandaise and a fluffy soufflé."

"Actually, the life you see now in Southern India has greatly improved since my youth," he continued. "As a child I remember seeing people die in the streets of hunger and disease. My family was always well off and we were never worried about our next meal, but you can't live among the homeless and the starving without becoming involved. Especially when you know that it is all so unnecessary. Such a damn waste!" He was silent for a while and then took out his handkerchief and blotted his dark brow. "There is so much undeveloped potential in India; for instance, here in Southern India our mills have removed the danger of starvation. Almost any man who is willing to work can eat and afford a place to stay. More people send their children to school. This would be good if only we had a meaningful education to offer them. If only we could shake off our stupid superstitions and cultural lags! Stupid!"

I decided that I would take advantage of what seemed to be one of Gupta's more pleasant moods. "But what about the dominant philosophy here, the acceptance of life as it is?" I asked.

"That sounds like a paraphrase of a freshman's analysis of Hinduism," he replied. "How ignorant you Westerners are of these beliefs. Of course one accepts—when one has no other choice. If a man can better himself, he does so. Only the holy man, who by some mystical means believes he knows the wish of God, would be willing to die of hunger without a battle. If you are really interested in the Indian, and for some strange reason I truly believe you are, observe him closely. Not with your Western eyes, but with empty, sensitive eyes. You'll find him like a child. Even the most humble and poor of them can find something to smile and laugh about. They seldom question. They are good workers. Perhaps, in a sense, they do accept, but only what is known and possible to them. I use 'them' because in a very real sense, I am not like them. I cannot be. I am not a Hindu. I have a Western education and my background is upper middle class."

We talked of many things that evening as another side of Gupta was revealed. He was interested, allowed me an opportunity to air my views and ask questions, and was much less abrupt than during our previous meetings.

"Let me help you to plan your trip through Southern India. First, I think you must see . . ." And so with Gupta's help, using Tiruchi as a base, I planned trips to the mill town of Ernakulum and the university town of Trivandrum.

In Trivandrum, I was asked to conduct a short seminar at one of the many universities for twelve graduate students in psychology, young men and women. Gupta had warned me, "Indian education is based upon the English system. That means that education is measured by the extent to which one is able to learn facts, not the meaning, just facts. Not the thinking processes, heaven forbid! It's a sad state of affairs. The student passes examinations, one after another, until he is finished with his formal education. Then he is graduated, but for nothing useful. He is at a loss as to what to do with the isolated facts he has learned. Most go to work for a bank or Shell Oil of India. It's a stupid shame!"

His analysis became dramatically apparent in my seminar. The students were intelligent and alert, knew all the facts, the labels, the definitions. They knew a great deal about the causes and treatment of mental illness, but confessed that they had never seen a real mental patient. I suggested that we visit a local mental hospital. They were first shocked, then intrigued by this proposal.

It was not surprising to find the mental hospital in Trivandrum suffering from the problems of such institutions throughout the world: it was overcrowded and understaffed, lacking both funds and professional help. The visit impressed some of the students deeply. Several felt that they might volunteer their help. They admitted, quite frankly, that they had never guessed their knowledge of psychology would ever have any real or practical value. Most of the students were from upper-class families where education was simply for its own sake. Several planned to join the family business, whatever that might be, while most of the girls would marry, run households.

Each day students came to my hotel to talk about their feelings and about the excitement of their new-found work at the institution. They generally agreed that Indian education, as it existed, had little, if any, effect whatsoever; that an educational revolution was the only hope for the

country's future, but still was a long way off. They were
eager for change, but had no idea from where it would
come. I was relieved that it would not be my responsibility.
We had problems enough in the United States with higher
education. The job seemed so great that it became easier to
understand why Gupta took refuge in feigned disinterest and
grumpy impatience.

"I'm happy you saw what you did," he said, when I
returned. "It's important that you know why we're moving so slowly. It's like the village women who are given
lectures on birth control. They listen attentively, then go
home and imagine that it did not pertain to them, that it
concerned only their neighbor, and go right on having children. I gave up years ago! It's very difficult to fight the
system. It's usually run by people who fear the new and
hold to the security of the old. The college here is small
but liberal. I try to use the American system, not the English.
I will not compromise my ideas. I make my students think.
I don't give one damn if they don't know the location of
Walden Pond as long as they know how Thoreau's philosophy applies to them. Damn heat!" he added, reaching for
his handkerchief.

I rested for a week in Cochin, a delightful city on the
Bay of Bengal. Like a tropical island, it was covered with
palm trees, flowers, and waterways of great beauty, fringed
by small, sparsely inhabited islands. One of the oldest cities
of India, it was an important port for centuries. The influ-
ence of the amalgamation of the cultures of many peoples
was still apparent: the Jews, the Christians, the Moslems,
the Hindus. Architecturally, it was a hodge-podge of Victorian buildings, 1950 modern and grass huts. Little boats
went from one wondrous island to another; vanishing into
jungle beauty, playing near clear deserted beaches, or past
parties of naked natives busily damming, cutting, or fishing

through tiny canals amid dense, wild patches of vegetation like abandoned gardens.

I went by waterway to the city of Ernakulum, and from there took a bus to Cape Comorin, where I sat among hundreds of awed observers on the vast sandy beach as the sun rose and set in the same rough, blue sea. Here, too, the mystical Temple of the Diamond Devi stood and defied the giant waves, its diamond headdress glittering magical rays out to sea and guiding the sailor safely home.

"I'm glad you think my country beautiful. But the finest of all the wonders of Southern India, as I told you, is the Temple of Madura," Gupta said, "that is, if you can ignore that damn paint job!" He gave me a letter to a professor at a medical school in Madura. "Samutri is an old friend. He will take good care of you."

I arrived by train in Madura, right at the scheduled time, as always. It was late afternoon, steamy and humid. Haze danced over the hot streets and even the flies had lost their vitality, resting quietly in the shadows, on huge dung heaps. The towers of the temple, visible from the train depot, were sun-yellow and deep purple in the distance. It was a simple process to find one's way in well-planned Madura. The temple was at the center of the city from which the roads paralleled, street by street, to the city limits.

At close range the temple was overpowering. Its four giant towers, each intricately carved with tiny figures of humans at work and play, rose like beacons over the city. The red and white painted outer wall contained several tall gates which gave access to the main inner chambers. Each chamber was vast and housed enormous statues of Gods. In the center court was a delicate reflecting pool, the largest in India. Inside, the worshippers moved in flowered splendor, traversing long hallways to enormous chambers, to intimate altars. Here and there sat gurus, surrounded by avid

pupils. Their lips moved slowly, softly, proudly and de-
votedly, articulating the ancient wisdom of the Gita or the
code of the Mahabarata, part of a religious heritage estab-
lished hundreds of years before the Christian era.

Stately priests with wise, dancing eyes blessed the eager
pilgrims gathered about them and performed their religious
rites with practiced agility.

Wedding parties accompanied by noisy bands and dancing transvestites moved through the crowds on their way to
all-night festivities.

Beggars sat in the coolness of the temple among animals
which yawned or defecated before giant altars as if the
temple had been built solely for their pleasure and use.

Odors of sandalwood, dung, incense, sweet-smelling
perfumes and human perspiration permeated the air.

Outside, the stairs led to the center court and the delicate
reflecting pool. It was crowded with half-naked throngs
busily preparing themselves for religious rituals, primping,
washing their clothes, simply basking in the sun, chatting
or cooling themselves half-submerged in the dirty, greenish
water.

Dr. Samutri's house was in what might be called the
suburbs since the more modern, larger homes were on the
outskirts of the town. He was expecting me.

"Oh, yes, you found us. Good. Come in. Gupta told us
you would be coming. Come in! Come in!" He was a large
muscular man in his forties, graying prematurely, with large
eyes, warm and vibrant. "This is my wife, Gretchen," introducing his blond, blue-eyed wife whom he had met while
studying in Vienna, "and our daughter, Lisa." Lisa was
perhaps the most beautiful child I had seen in my travels,
with the best features of both handsome parents.

When I was seated they gathered eagerly about me. "We
are dying of curiosity. How on earth did you ever meet

Gupta? He's such a loner. I never thought he ever spoke to anyone, least of all a stranger. He seems to have such a keen interest in you. His letter was glowing. What is it?"

I described our meeting. "I really don't know why he has been so kind. He's been great."

Samutri laughed. "Gupta has become a romanticist in his old age. An Indian at last. He really is a good chap, you know. It is just that he is rather a snob. People fear him a bit and don't relish having him around. Happily for him, he enjoys being alone. One must know him before his real charm and sense of humor can be appreciated."

"We love him," Gretchen laughed. "We find him so refreshing. He hates everything so. Actually, he is the warmest person we know. I call him the Indian Robert Morley. He looks like him, don't you think? All those chins, the sour expression covering the puckish look, the way he swaggers when he walks."

"He claims he hates India," Samutri cut in. "He calls the Indians by his favorite expression, 'stupid.' Actually, he loves his country. It is just that he feels frustrated. Like so many of us who have seen the world, Gupta and I would like to shove our people out of their dormant state. But we find that to wake someone who has been asleep in the cool shadows for so long is not easy. We have to be patient. We must be willing to offer him time. Gupta has no patience, so it drives him mad! You know, he could get a position almost anywhere in India if he were willing to put up with the system, but he choses to make less money and live amid the discomforts of Tiruchi for the freedom of living and teaching what and how he pleases. There are many like him in India. Abhorred by the sophisticated Indian because he makes him look at himself, feared by the poor Indian because he will not be pushed. So Gupta exists in a world apart. But what about you?"

That evening we had Weiner schnitzel for dinner, then went to the roof of the house where we sat on a swing and listened to Beethoven's Ninth Symphony while watching the mystical Madura Temple change colors with the approaching night.

My final stops were in Madras, Bangalore and Mysore. As Gupta had said, they were the three most physically beautiful cities in the South of India. All offered the old and the new in pleasant, flowered surroundings: ancient weed-vine covered temples and shrines, together with patterned, pampered gardens. Simple shacks crumbled in the shadows of maharajas' vast marbled palaces. Vendors with dime store trinkets sat on boxes in front of luxurious shops selling jewelry of solid gold and precious stones, available on credit.

On my return to Tiruchi, I informed Gupta that it would be necessary for me to move on. He seemed strangely different to me now and it had become easier to ignore his peculiar mannerisms, his odd outbursts and his wicked lashing tongue.

"So," he said, "how did you find Southern India? Did you discover the mystery and glamour you came to find or was it just a dirty, overcrowded bore?"

I am sure I sensed true pride in his expression as I spoke of my strong attraction to his country, its art, its culture, but especially its people.

"Yes, India is beautiful but it's changing," he said. "From the untouchable who still wanders the streets in his nakedness, sore-infested and sick, to the rich mill owner who sits on his fan-cooled veranda and complains about taxation, we are all changing. From the maharaja, looking back to the time when his dilapidated marble palace was stacked with chests of precious jewels and crowded with elegant maharanies, to the field worker and the rising white-collar worker, we all are having to face this change, each in his own way. No one can escape it. But it's so damn *slow*, this process." He mopped his brow. "The hell with it!" he said. "Anyway, I'm happy you came to the south and we have become friends." He mumbled this in a rather embarrassed manner, staring at his rings.

The last time I saw Gupta, he was mopping his brow furiously and cursing the station porter for handling my luggage so carelessly. "Stupid man!" he said in English. "When will these people wake up?"

chapter 10

Calcutta

Don't spend your precious time asking "Why isn't the world a better place?" It will only be time wasted. The question to ask is "How can I make it better?" To that question, there is an answer.

The Case Family

On first impression, Calcutta seems to be the most crowded, dirtiest, ugliest and most depressing city in India. It has neither monument, nor fresh sea, nor beautiful garden, nor fantastic temple, nor obvious rich culture to recommend it. It is large, sprawled out, a colorless industrial city where the air is heavy with dust, smoke and stench. Sacred cow and naked child defecate in the main street; crowds move indifferently through throngs of starving, maimed, crippled beggars. Autos, buses and taxis speed through garbage-infested streets with equal indifference toward stray child, lame old man or dog. The sun beats down unmercifully most of the year, drying the land so that even the open spaces seem like vast deserts; the river flows through the city black with oil and smelly debris. The lawns of the parks are dirt-dust brown and the trees cry for attention, punishing those who ignore their need with little shade.

It is a city of great wealth and desperate poverty, of great concern and callous indifference, of great promise and lack of all hope, of over-fed and starving, of silk saris and shriveled peasant nakedness. It is a city where, daily, endless streams of hopeless humanity wind their way, fighting for a section of sidewalk or deserted road on which to settle their tired bodies.

Calcutta is India in transition, the India of the intellectual, the new thinker, the West; like the Chicago of the twenties, Paris of the eighteen hundreds, Naples of the forties. Whatever else it is, Calcutta is not basking in the decaying ruins or the fly-infested dung heaps. It is moving.

The day I arrived in Calcutta was a scorching, hazy, dusty one, when all activity seems forced and frantic, when people, hot and sticky, feel maximum indifference.

Although I had written to the YMCA well in advance, I was informed that they had no reservation for me and had no time to answer requests for rooms. It was suggested that I go down the road to a church hostel. Perhaps they would have something, if I were not too particular.

Back on the street, I was immediately surrounded by a mass of beggars, by those who wanted to direct me, to carry my luggage, to introduce me to a house of prostitution. Twisted figures, faceless, voiceless, squirmed about me like hungry sidewalk reptiles.

"Baksheesh! (Money!)" they moaned.

The walk to the hostel became a nightmare. I gathered beggars like a pied piper and found myself becoming vicious and cursing at them to leave me alone, which they refused to do. Even my light suitcase weighed upon me and prevented my pushing my way past the group.

The flight of steps leading to the hostel seemed to act as an artificial barrier, causing the beggars to scatter and vanish as mysteriously as they had appeared.

In a small room at the top of the stairs, at an old Victorian desk, sat a very young, very dark Indian boy.

"Do you have a room?" I asked.

"I call Miss Case, Sahib," he said, and vanished through a strangely decorated dining room. It was a large room, dark and cluttered with assorted odd pieces of furniture. The room opened onto a balcony which overlooked the narrow street below. It seemed cooler here.

After a few minutes the boy reappeared.

"Miss Case come soon, Sahib. You wait, please."

He stared at me innocently. To break what seemed to me an awkward silence, I smiled at him and asked, "Have you lived in Calcutta long?"

He smiled a large white-toothed smile, "All the life."

At that moment Mrs. Case appeared. She was overpowering, at least as tall as I and twice as heavy, a solid, firm heaviness. Her light hair was cut in a mannish bob, short and combed straight back over her head, accentuating a long, rather sensitive face and deep blue eyes. Her voice was low-pitched and her inflection was almost unfriendly.

"I'd like a room," I said. "The YMCA suggested that I come here in the hope that you might have a place for me to stay."

"I have a room," she said, matter-of-factly, with an American accent. "How long will you be?"

"I don't know; I have no particular schedule."

"It doesn't matter."

She handed me a large book and asked me to register. "Remember, this is not a luxury hotel. You will have to 'do' for yourself except for meals. The food is Indian and you may have to share your room."

"This is a non-profit hostel," she continued, "as it is, we just manage to keep open from day to day. We're here primarily as a mission."

In fluent Bengali she instructed the boy where to take me.

We crossed the dining room into a hall and ascended a very narrow wooden staircase. The boy opened the door, which had no lock, and led me into the room. It had two beds and a small dresser. The walls were of stucco, clean and plain. On the dresser was a Bible, the only item other than the basic furniture. There was one small window which looked directly into an apartment house just a few yards away, where smoke rose seemingly from nowhere, as if the rooms were on fire.

Then I was guided up another long flight of stairs to a bathroom. Again, no frills: sink, a clean but broken mirror which distorted everything, a shower head reaching out like a thin, wrecked arm from one wall, and a Western-style toilet bowl with no seat.

I expressed my mixed pleasure to the boy with a "Namaste" and a broad smile and returned to my room.

"Dinner start at seven, Sahib," he informed me, closing the door behind him.

It quickly became apparent that my first impression of the room's coolness was only due to the contrast with the intense heat outside; I could feel beads of perspiration forming over my back and running slowly down my body in trickling streams. I removed my clothes and dried myself with a towel, to no avail; in a few moments I was again dripping wet.

It was now late afternoon and I prepared to go out into the city. Certainly Calcutta had more to offer than the horror I had seen in the few streets I had walked.

I started out through the dining room. Two boys were busily setting tables for dinner. One I recognized as the boy who had greeted me upon my arrival. He brightened up.

"Doctor," he shouted, "you doctor? You write doctor on book."

"Yes," I said, "I'm a doctor."

"You help me please," he said and led me into the adjoining kitchen. As he began to undo his trousers it occurred to me that he thought I was a physician.

"No," I said, "not that kind of doctor. I am a doctor of philosophy."

It was no use. His trousers were down around his ankles exposing his extremely thin trunk, sunken stomach and long, dark, spindly legs. He ran his fingers through his pubic hair and pointed out tiny red bites, indicating his discomfort by going through the motions of scratching, then looked at me questioning. It was easy for even a layman to diagnose crabs, and anyone who had traveled through the Orient, staying in small local hotels and hostels, was normally well equipped to handle them. I smiled. "I cannot show Mama Case," he said simply. "You have medicine?"

I indicated that he should pull up his trousers and come with me. We returned to my room where I gave him the necessary instructions and the bottle of liquid which I carried.

"Namaste, doctor," he said.

I walked out into the blinding afternoon. The sun was hotter than ever. Crowds of unwashed and dirty people moved slowly through the streets, seemingly without direction.

Most of the streets were narrow, dusty and littered with the accumulated trash of weeks.

I moved amid stalls and past walls lined with vendors. Children were engaged in the game of begging. They followed for blocks whining "baksheesh" with dirty palms extended, and seemed to revel in the irritation they produced, growing ever more aggressive and pleased with themselves. Suddenly I was confronted with a tall, rather impressive building, the Calcutta Opera House. It faced a large covered market offering everything from the finest silks to the most base, twisted sweet potatoes. With everyone engaged in bargaining, searching and shouting, it was very much like other Asian markets, only perhaps more congested, unkempt, filthy and smelly.

Strangely patterned streets took me past long queues waiting before hundreds of movie houses blaring dissonant music and covered by advertising placards showing richly-garbed, heavily-jeweled and painted maharanies with their handsome maharajas. I finally emerged into a large open space which I recognized as Victoria Square. The streets around the square were lined by shops, restaurants and the more expensive, air-conditioned movie houses with shorter queues.

The park only suggested what it was intended to be. Its grass had given way to dirt from misuse and lack of water. Sacred cows moved slowly across the dry field, searching dumbly for something, seemingly not certain what. Groups of people huddled around, on the dirt, talking, selling, buying.

At one end of the square was a row of buildings, black with soot and dust and the terminal for noisy streetcars. At the opposite end was the Victoria Goverment House, before which passed busy streets and tram tracks, leading to the river and beyond.

I started back to the hostel slowly; both because of the intense heat which precluded speed and the deep depression the city had imposed upon me.

When I arrived, dinner was already being served. I sat at one of the unoccupied tables, but was shortly asked to join the group at a table near the balcony.

"It's cooler here," a fair man with a British accent told me.

He introduced me to the others, all of whom were staying as guests of the hostel. Two were missionaries visiting Calcutta for just a few days from an area near Hyderabad in central India. There was an English family, husband, wife and two teen-aged boys, who had once lived in India and were now visiting with friends and feeling rather nostalgic about the "old" way. The other member of the group was a rather plain young girl from an American university, who was touring India to research the dissertation she was writing on comparative religions.

"How long have you been in India?"

"Several months."

"How long will you stay?"

The routine questioning.

"I don't know."

"Do you like it?"

"I loved the south and central parts," I said, "I could have stayed in Cochin, Ernakulum, Trivandrum, Cape Comorin or even Madura forever. I like the central part, too, but I'm not sure, if Calcutta is typical, that I shall love the North."

"Give it a chance," said the plain girl. "It's glorious! So fantastically alive and earthy."

"Rather too alive and earthy for my taste," the Englishman with the family commented dryly. "It's changed since the war. Funny, but it's rather the way a house changes when the builders move."

"The builders!" the young minister exclaimed. "Do you mean we British? You know, though it's apparently still not understood by some of our countrymen, the Indians were here even before the British."

The American student laughed gaily. None of the others joined her and she became quiet.

The conversation safely returned to me as we ate.

"Are you going to the service?"

"I wasn't planning to," I answered.

"You should go at least once," the American girl said. "You must see Mrs. Case work. It's a real experience."

After dinner, I joined the English family and we descended the stairs to the street level. We walked up a dirt drive to a large hall where the service was to be held.

In a room completely devoid of furniture or ornament, at least fifty Indians, perhaps more, were seated cross-legged, hungrily eating rice and curds with their fingers off sections of banana leaves. Two Indian boys scurried among them with pots of food and with agile movements poured second helpings of food onto the small shiny leaves.

As those present finished their meal, the boys gathered the leaves, depositing them in a large cardboard box which they dragged from the room. Everyone then settled themselves, facing now in one direction, and waited. After a moment, Mrs. Case appeared. She wore a white robe and, over it, a heavy cape of black.

The room was hot and smelled of sweating, unwashed bodies and food. Mrs. Case's forehead was covered with dots of perspiration but she appeared cool and comfortable. In one hand she carried a Bible which she did not open. She stood before them and began to speak with smooth, caressing ease, in what I surmised was the Bengali dialect.

They sat before her in silence and deep respect. It was not clear from their expressionless faces whether they understood her or not. The English family seemed to understand what she was saying and responded every now and then with a murmured "Amen, sister," but no one else seemed particularly to hear.

After ten minutes, Mrs. Case smiled, folded her hands in a "Namaste" sign over the Bible and walked into the group. The listeners rose, adjusting their clothes which were stuck to their skin by sweat. When the last of them had gone, Mrs. Case walked over to us, greeted the English family, and smiled at me. She seemed softer, kinder, than she had that afternoon.

"I'm glad you came," she said. "I understand you are a physician."

"No, I'm a Ph.D."

"Oh, I'm sorry," she said, "I thought I could put you to work if you were a real doctor. There's not much use for another Ph.D. here. There's enough philosophy already in India. Too much, in fact!"

She wiped her brow. "It's not much cooler outside," she said, "but if you have no other plans, would you like to join me for a stroll?"

The English family excused themselves and we walked together into the humid night. The sun was gone but its heat remained.

"It's been a hot day," she said, fanning herself with her handkerchief. We walked for some distance in silence.

"Vishnu said you gave him some medicine," she said.

"Not medicine, really," I answered. "He has crabs. I gave him something that will take care of them. I told him I'm not a medical doctor, but he doesn't seem to accept the fact."

She laughed, a deep-throated laughter. "How could you ever expect someone like Vishnu to understand? He saw your signature in the book, and it said 'Doctor.' As far as he is concerned, there is only one kind of doctor."

As we continued our walk, she asked me none of the usual questions: Why was I traveling? Did I like India? How long would I be there?

When we arrived at the river, she led me to a small boat landing. The street lights were on, with neon signs on the buildings advertising Coca Cola, shoes, silks. The air was no cooler but seemed fresher. Night color swept Calcutta clean, and the young people walking along the bank and in the surrounding shadows might have been lovers in any of the world's large cities. Cars and motorcycle cabs putted by, while the inevitable pimps and prostitutes sauntered alone, conspicuously, slowly.

"This is the only time this poor city is beautiful, when it takes on the color of the night," she sighed. She was very relaxed, woman-like.

We talked for a long time.

"My husband and I came here more than twenty years ago from Iowa. He was newly ordained. We were in the south of India near Poona," she told me. "It was beautiful there. Actually, we didn't do much converting, but when people are sick and hungry there isn't much time for preaching. I hated India at first, but there is something very special about it. From the way you spoke a little while ago, I think you know what I mean. It creates an excitement, a passion, that makes one more aware of life." She looked into the swiftly moving black river.

"My husband died in Poona. Some strange disease. Actually, I think it was more like a depression. He was a big man, even bigger than I. Football player and all that, but underneath he was too soft. I think he found the task too great and his contribution too small. I think he just gave up one day and died. At first, I thought I'd go home, to the States, but then I heard about this mission in Calcutta. The people who had been running it just quit. They couldn't seem to understand the Indians. They kept feeling they should want to help themselves! People assured me it would be better for me to be in a city like Calcutta, but I think

India is fine almost anywhere for a woman alone. Here it's not the rapists and thieves who keep you off the streets, but the beggars. Anyway, I find that after a while the beggars get to know you and leave you alone. They are a pretty smart lot, especially the children and the cripples. Some say that they are the only ones, except the rich, who eat regularly in Calcutta."

We wandered back to the hostel. At times it was necessary for us to walk in the street for the sidewalks had become the hotels of the poor, and for blocks in all directions they were lying along the road, grouped together like rows of corpses.

"How can the officials keep Calcutta clean, or any other city in India for that matter? When almost one-third of the city's population uses the sidewalks for their home, when the streets become their kitchens, their garbage cans, their toilets?" As she spoke, we turned into the hostel drive. Vishnu and three other boys were seated on the steps.

"Namaste, Doctor," Vishnu said. Mrs. Case and I laughed.

Early the next morning Vishnu knocked on my door. "Sahib," he said, "I bring two friends to see you." He entered with two Indian boys in their early twenties. "They need doctor. You look see." He spoke to the boys. One lifted the shirt which hung over his dhoti and exposed huge sores, pus-filled and inflamed. The other loosened his dhoti to display a large, chancrous penis.

"Much hurt," said Vishnu, the self-appointed Florence Nightingale.

I knew there was no use in trying to explain that I was not a physician so I asked them to return in a few hours. I showered. I ate my breakfast. Vishnu served me with great pleasure. Obviously he considered me a godsend, and it became apparent that I was given more of everything being served. He loved the title, "Doctor," using it at every opportunity.

After breakfast, I gathered up Vishnu's two friends and set out to find a physician. I found one on the main square, an English-speaking Indian with accent and bedside manner imported directly from London's West End. After I explained the situation to him, his initial response was to direct me to the nearest dispensary. The two boys, not understanding a word, stood by nervously. At last he agreed to look at them. He did not speak to either, but conducted both examinations roughly, forgetting his smooth manner. Finally, he wrote prescriptions for both and told them what they had to do. He also instructed them to go to the dispensary in the future.

Later that afternoon Vishnu came to see me. "Why not you take care of friends?"

I felt that I should stop this at once, before I found myself "doctor" to all the infirm of Calcutta, a tall order for even a massive team of physicians. Through gestures and simple words I told him that I could not treat anyone, that all my tools and medicines were back in the United States and that he should tell his friends they need not fear the dispensary, that care there was good—and free. He listened to my explanation with only a degree of acceptance.

Each day Calcutta grew more hot and seemingly more crowded. Thousands of immigrants arrived daily and there seemed no way to stop the flow. Small tents of rags were set up in almost every open space; after nine in the evening, the sidewalks were almost impassable. The city stifled me. I longed for an open space, a single moment of silence and peace, a tree, or something that was clean and dust-free or beautiful.

One afternoon I met a wealthy Indian in a theater where I had gone to escape the terrible heat. He was a very kind man and was most interested in my reactions to India. We spent several evenings in his garden-surrounded, fan-cooled home, talking about birth control, relief for the needy, medical care for the sick; but the magnitude of these problems was so great that every attempt toward their solution was very much like killing a single flea on the tail of a giant elephant. Our talks, though interesting, always left me somewhat ill at ease, confused and frustrated.

But Mrs. Case obviously felt that something could be done. Her days were full. In the early morning she set out on her daily trek to solicit help from the more fortunate. "Indians who have money never refuse a Westerner who is begging," she told me. "They give almost freely as if by giving they are passing some of the responsibility on to someone else and alleviating their own frustrations and guilt." With this money in her hand, and accompanied by her four adopted sons, headed by Vishnu, she would shout her way to bargains in the marketplace. Here she was known as "Miss Case of the loud voice and the strong arms," but she was obviously well loved.

Upon arriving home, she fed her hostel guests, helped to keep the place in order, supervised the work and the daily menu and finally set to the task of cooking for the fifty or sixty hungry street dwellers she would gather up for the evening meal.

The fact that she was feeding the poor was well known throughout Calcutta, and some of the hungry were always assembled at the dinner hour, waiting for what would be their only meal of the day.

"First you feed their empty bellies, then you preach to their minds. I'm sure half of them don't understand my Iowa Bengali. But they sit quietly and they are fed and that's really all that matters, isn't it?"

As the days passed my feelings about Calcutta changed.

I no longer felt horror at the sights I saw, merely defeat. The beggars no longer bothered me, I simply ignored their terrible whines and pleading cries. Even the heat felt almost pleasant when one stopped trying to fight it.

Finally, I told Mrs. Case I was leaving. She seemed unhappy. "I'm sorry to see you go. I thought you might end up being another of our crazy crusaders, but I guess you see the joke of it all," she said. "I know I'm not *really* doing anything important, but I feel that just to keep forty or fifty people alive for one more day is something. Who knows the answer?"

She looked at me apologetically, almost ashamed.

When I left, Mrs. Case and her family lined up to say goodbye. Vishnu did not understand why I was leaving after so few days.

"I'm a coward," I said. He looked puzzled.

I avoided looking at Mrs. Case when I shook her hand; I picked up my suitcase and left quickly.

chapter 11

Kashmir

To see people as they really are we must love them unconditionally. Unless we do so, they may not reveal themselves to us and we will miss them forever.

Katie

We were told that due to the severity of the weather no flights had been able to complete the trip from Delhi to Srinigar during recent weeks. Srinigar, situated as it is, surrounded by gigantic mountains, had been snowed in and was inaccessible. However, most of the well-dressed passengers had come at least halfway around the world to know, firsthand, the mystery of the Valley of Kashmir, and the flight was full.

One passenger stood out among the rest. She was in her middle twenties, wearing a black angora turtleneck sweater, far too large for her and too warm for the climate. It hung loosely over her thin body and clung to her wide hips and thighs. Tight-fitting ski pants covered her plump legs. On her large unkempt and unwashed feet were loose Indian sandals that slapped the floor when she walked. Her hair, predominantly blond, hung in multi-colored tangles as if it hadn't been brushed in days. Her nose was too long and

too pointed, her lips too thin; her face plain, pale and showing no sign of care or makeup. She was obviously alone,
oblivious and unconcerned.

When our flight was announced, most of the passengers,
in pairs or groups, rushed to be first on board. After the
scramble was over, I boarded and found myself sitting next
to Katie.

She was an English sociologist, she told me, on a tour
of India, studying the effects of English colonization on the
Indian. After this short, polite identification, she seemed to
have nothing else to say and no desire to continue the conversation. The trip was made in silence. She all but buried
herself in her book.

By the time the plane was approaching the mountains,
the weather had become impossibly rough forcing us to land
at a small airport at the base of the mountains. The passengers were incensed upon hearing the announcement that
we could either reboard the plane for a return flight to Delhi,
stay there at the airline's expense on the chance that the
weather would clear the following day or take the local
bus on to Srinigar. The storms in the mountains were re-
ported to be so violent that there was some question whether
even the bus would be able to make the trip.

"You must take us there! We came all the way from
Ohio."

"This is unforgivable, it's the height of inefficiency. I'll
speak to the French Consul about this. This is no way to
treat a French tourist."

"This would never have happened if the incompetent
Indians were still under us British, I tell you."

"But I'm on a tight schedule, I can't wait."

Having thus expressed their indignation, the passengers
all decided to return to Delhi, and still grumbling, filed back

to the plane. I was determined to try the next day; if this were impossible, I had decided to trust the bus.

The airplane motors sputtered insecurely and the plane took off and vanished into the gathering black clouds.

I turned back toward the building. There, squatted against the wall like a thin black spider, was the only other remaining passenger, Katie, still calmly reading her book.

"You decided to stay, too?" I asked rather stupidly.

She looked up from her book, squinted and smiled. "I decided that back in England."

The airline agent, a dark, stout Indian with a clipped British accent, drove us to the hotel over a roughly paved road.

"This is not Delhi," he explained superfluously, obviously annoyed at the inconvenience which our remaining there would cause him.

The one main road of the city was lined with the usual open-front shops, made beautiful with multi-colored materials hanging in broad drapes from the ceilings, and piles of hand-crafted materials in shining brass, copper and stone. Small roads with residences of stone, wood or stucco led in straight lines off the main street and up the hills which framed the village. Above the town stood a massive mosque, like a huge copper monster, with thin armlike minarets raised to heaven asking protection for the infant city curled in the lap of the mountain. We were now in Moslem country.

The desk clerk assured us that although the hotel was not like those in Delhi, rooms would be readied for us. The rooms were enormous: each with a sink, a private toilet and windows which overlooked the residential area of the city. The beds were Western-style with mattresses caved in at the middle and brown with use.

"Well," said the agent, "I told you it wasn't Delhi. You must take your meals at the restaurant across the road."

Sparsely-clad servants moved leisurely about: Katie lay quietly on her unmade bed, watching them intently with her small, bright eyes. "Aren't they wonderful people?" she commented when I looked in on her. "Even the poorest and the most uneducated Indian seems to have his own private world which he shares with no one. A hundred million mysteries." She watched them for a few moments in silence.

"Look at the way they clean the dresser. I'm sure they think it's an ornament, never used inside. I noticed a maggoty bowl of rice in the drawer. I'll bet they don't even think of opening a drawer." We watched until the servants left. The room was quite clean, the maggots undisturbed. "Ha! Just as I told you. Isn't that wonderful?" she laughed gaily and bounced on the bed. It was a fine laugh, unaffected, intelligent, warm.

The rest of the afternoon we walked through the narrow streets of the city. Most of the time we were silent. Katie, in her spider-like garb, drew more than casual attention from the Indians, who, with child-like curiosity, stared as we passed. Naked children followed us up the streets, laughing and chattering among themselves until they lost interest, then disappeared down another noisy road to find their way home.

We stayed up late, watching the color of the city fade into cold night and talked.

Katie questioned everything but wanted answers to nothing. She wondered if there were any answers at all. She struggled with the need to free herself from her own culture in order to truly see, feel and understand India.

"I feel as if I have lived here before. Perhaps in another life," she mused.

"In spite of poverty, illness, wars, political and religious differences, the Indian has somehow managed to hold onto what life is all about," she continued softly. "There is such a reverence for life, as if each day one walked the path from birth, at dawn, to death, at night, only to be reborn the following day."

"They have a very different concept of love and beauty, you know. Heavens! They see beauty even in me. I always thought I was one of the few girls who could travel all over the world and be as safe as I am in England. Even Italians don't pinch me. But, God, I found I was wrong about that in India. They think I'm great. For an Indian, love and sex are very different things. Very uncomplicated," she snapped her fingers simply. "I have been in India a year and I have been proposed to by hotel clerks and bus drivers, propositioned by businessmen and policemen, and seduced by a man who claimed that he was the Maharaja of Jaipur. I knew differently, of course, but it was a great seduction. And such romantics! They weep with passion and joy. They love to give flowery speeches. Really, quite grand."

It was a strange, wonderful night. We found that we were communicating, enjoying that rare experience of finding another human being who hears you. I soon realized that Katie was much like the India she loved—poor, unkempt, ragged, but unconcerned, and full of the beauty and vitality of life.

In the morning the hotel manager awakened me to report that the plane was not even going to leave Delhi, the flight had been permanently cancelled, and that if we hurried we would still have time to catch the bus.

Katie was already up and sitting outside in the cold morning air, absorbed in her book. She looked less tired than the previous day, but just as unkempt.

"Have you heard?" she asked. "I think the bus will be a lot more fun anyway, don't you?"

News travels fast in small Indian villages and before we could leave for the bus station, a new Mercedes drove up and a fat, rather pleasant-looking Indian stepped out. He bowed, "Allow me to introduce myself. I am Mr. Atal," he said. "I am on my way to Srinigar by car. I have business there. Business, you can be sure, is not ruled by weather," he continued in a clipped British accent. "I must be in Srinigar by this evening. I heard that you were looking for a ride. May I have the honor of offering you the comforts of my car? It will be company for me and for you it will be superior to the bus which is dirty and very cold."

An almost disappointed Katie, after looking at me in desperation and finding no escape, nodded her consent and we took our places in the luxurious car. Mr. Atal seated himself between Katie and me, with his daughter who was accompanying him, on his lap. He held her small body close like a lover; she folded herself, like a limp doll, to the contours of his pudgy body and remained awake but silent, only moving occasionally to readjust her long, neatly-tied braids.

The road was in terrible condition, the weather vile, and the trip took almost fourteen hours. We seemed to wind endlessly through one mountain range after another. Mr. Atal talked continuously of everything from his love of mother England to literature and religion, emphasizing that he was a Christian.

A few times we stopped for tea in very small villages. Mr. Atal had obviously passed this way often and was well known. His manner was always curt and his tone one of impatience. "These biscuits are stale! Take them away! Can't serve the tea hot? Do you not know how to make tea yet?" He would turn to us: "You must forgive these people, they are truly uncivilized. True civilization left India with the British. Now we are left with pseudo-sophisticated bores and dull-witted peasants!"

Except for a few pleasantries, Katie said not a word during the entire trip.

The roads through the mountains became more icy. Icicles hung from roofs and electric wires and snow covered the mountains and fields in all directions. The lakes were mostly frozen and showed gray beneath the crisp, now moonlit, sky as we arrived in Srinigar.

"Where will you stay?" Mr. Atal asked.

"On a houseboat," Katie and I answered, almost together.

"A houseboat? That is no place to stay in mid-winter. You will freeze to death; besides, they are all closed."

Eventually he realized that we would neither accept his invitation to stay in his twelve-room house, which he generously offered, nor move into the city's one open Western-style hotel. He shrugged indifference and ordered his driver to pull over beside the low stone wall which edged the lake. He wrapped a heavy blanket around him and stepped out into the night. "Houseboat!" he called impatiently into the darkness.

At once the night became alive with lights, lanterns and small boats. These soon formed at the foot of a series of steps. Mr. Atal stood above the assembly like a general addressing his troops. After a few moments, he returned climbing back into the car and slamming the door loudly against the cold.

"Habib is a good houseboat manager, he will let you have his best boat for a bit more than two dollars American or," to Katie, "one pound English, a day for the two of you. That, of course, includes all meals, a houseboy, and a cook, and Habib himself will be your guide as part of the price."

We removed our suitcases from the trunk, and after offering our thanks and a brief goodbye, we stumbled down the steep steps to be greeted by Habib, holding a lantern.

He was of medium height, dark, mustached, rather plump.

He had a happy smile that showed his pride at having been chosen from all the other houseboat owners, who stood about in frustrated defeat, to house such illustrious guests at such an out-of-season time.

He rowed us to his boat. "This is My Sunshine, my finest houseboat," he said. "My brother and me own four boats, but this is the best of all. It will not take too long to get it ready. I will get the cook to make you some tea while you wait. You will be pleased with my boat."

The houseboy met us at the cabin door. He was barefoot. The upper part of his body was covered with an old green pullover under a loose, white jacket, and a white dhoti hung below his thin waist. He took our bags into the living room, where he started a fire in a large pot-bellied stove. Habib had vanished, and Katie and I were alone.

"A houseboat in Kashmir," she exulted. "Old Katie has made it at last! I couldn't care less if we froze to death here. Isn't it grand? God! The thought of staying with Mr. Industrialist, saved Christian, expert in philosophy, culture and the living arts made me cringe."

But Mr. Atal had been right. It was freezing cold, but at the moment that seemed unimportant, for the boat was a true beauty. We examined every inch. The living room was large and Victorian in decoration. The furniture was heavy and formal but comfortable. In the center of the room was the large wood stove, now rumbling with fire-life. Lace curtains hung from the windows and drooped to touch spectacular, soft Kashmir rugs of intricate pattern and rich color.

All along the port side of the boat ran a narrow passage, which gave access to the many rooms, including a dining room furnished with a heavy, carved table and chairs of oak. Separated from the dining room by an ornate door was the kitchen where we could hear Habib talking softly with the houseboy or cook. Adjacent to the dining room were two

large bedrooms, each with double beds and separate bath-
rooms containing huge sinks and baths. It was true luxury.

The houseboy served us English tea, strong, hot and
welcome. Habib, who had returned, sat cross-legged on the
living room rug in his loose flowing trousers and tent-like
wool coat, beneath which he held his individual fire pot,
providing him with his own built-in heating system.

"You both must have such coats. Then I'll give you fire
pots like mine and you will always be warm."

Tired, but too excited for sleep, we sat by the stove and
talked late into the night. Habib, like all the Kashmiri, was
Moslem. Although India was his country, the mountains
and the religion made Kashmir a separate world. He was
completely different from the Hindus I had known.

"I shall take you everywhere," he promised. "I am free.
I have much time. In the summer and spring, life is very
busy. Wealthy people from Delhi come to Kashmir, but
they are very difficult to please. I prefer to have foreigners
on my boats. They are more easy to make happy. Tomorrow
we shall see many things. First, we shall make you coats
so that you will be warm. It will be cold for many months
yet. Why did you not come in the summer? It is most
beautiful in the summer, when all is garden. But you will
find it nice now, too. This is the time when the city again
belongs to its people. We shall have many good times," he
said. "How long will you stay?"

"We don't know yet," I answered. "We shall see. Is that
all right?"

"All is all right," he replied. Thus assured, we slept well
that night.

The following days were clouded over by a dream-like,
gray-white haze that settled over the lake and sliced the
surrounding mountains in two. Occasionally, patches of
blue sky became suddenly visible; then, from between

mountain peaks, black clouds would move silently into the valley and drop their pale gray-white moisture over the city.

I had a coat made, as Habib suggested. It had a small collar which buttoned tightly at the neck, then fell like a large tent to below the knees. Katie insisted that she did not need one but was finally persuaded to drape a long wool blanket over her turtleneck sweater, changing her spider-like garb to that of a brown-winged lady bug. We were supplied with fire pots which we were instructed to carry under our coats above stomach level which made us both look nine months pregnant. But, as everyone in Srinigar carried fire pots, we were no more conspicuous than the others.

We spent our days eating wonderfully exotic foods, huddled around the wood stove in our living room; sailing with Habib over the rippleless, icy, gray lake and narrow canals; strolling through the maze of wooden structures, stores, stalls, temples and mosques which made up the city; walking under trees whose giant branches hung nakedly above the muddy streets and through large gardens which revealed only a skeletal suggestion of the multi-colored lushness of the summer and spring to come.

The streets were always marvels of activity. In spite of the cold and the constantly falling mist or snow, they were crowded and alive with ghost-like white-garbed women and drably-dressed men, bulging with fire pots. The children seemed like children the world over, oblivious to the weather as they ran, dashed and screamed between the crowds through the crowded narrow streets. All this was the Kashmir we had become so much a part of.

Spice stalls full of bags, bottles, and shiny tins containing powders, seeds and acrid spices offered a spectrum of colors and odors which Katie pecked at like a little bird. Though it was impossible to question or discuss sensation with the vendors, our expressions and gestures provided the necessary communication. "You must taste this," gestured the storekeeper. "It's very bitter," answered Katie's expression.

Families of rug makers were huddled together behind paper thin walls, their agile fingers flying over intricate patterns which would soon become expensive Kashmiri rugs. We listened in icy silence as the leader chanted the colors to be added in a dull sing-song voice and the half-frozen group responded in conditioned, unquestioning silence to his commands, still in ignorance of what the final results would be.

Katie was a worshipper of the senses. Things were not real, did not exist, until she had smelled, felt and tasted them. At times she seemed almost mesmerized, entranced, by the feel of a deep wool rug or the odors drifting from earthen pots of hot food steaming over crackling fires along the road.

"The city seemed, at first, washed water gray," she commented one day, "as if its colors were all resting for the winter on the clouds of the mountains, but now it shimmers red and orange everywhere."

At night Habib would join us in the living room. Katie would curl up, cat-like, on the heavy couch or sit on the floor and pull her large legs up under her chin. With the wind tossing the rain softly against the window, we would talk about many things.

"But we were promised," Habib would say. "They said that after the emergency we could decide either to remain as part of India or go with Pakistan. There is no doubt that the decision was made a long time ago. We are Moslems, we are not Hindus. It is only that we live in India, but we are not truly Indians. Yet we must be silent and not talk about it."

It was during this conversation that we learned of Habib's

brother, Alam. Alam was a radical, a deeply religious man who was determined that Kashmir, which seemed more their homeland than did India, must become a part of Pakistan. He was an expert on the Koran and believed this change was preordained. He was deeply respected in the valley.

In her quiet way, Katie revealed a deep knowledge and understanding of the politics and religions of India. Habib and Alam were constantly caught off guard by her ability to quote directly from the Koran and her keen interpretation of the words she quoted as by her general knowledge of their country and its social and political history.

Alam joined us in our evening talks. He was very thin, pale-faced, with sunken deep-black eyes, a mass of even deeper black hair and a several days' growth of beard. His lips were heavy and moved slowly around the English words which he pronounced with great care. Some evenings he would read to us softly, in Arabic, the holy words of the Koran. As he read, the language sounded like a soothing morning raga.

Though he had a great disdain for women generally, Alam's respect for Katie grew. After several evening discussions, he began to look upon her as almost his equal and used her to supply the knowledge which he so eagerly wanted in the areas of psychology, philosophy and the social systems of the world.

"Are people truly free?"

"How can it be that all men are equal?"

"Is it true that you believe in one God, and that you believe He is the *only* God for all men on earth?"

He listened closely to Katie's intelligent, simple answers. His black eyes became even darker and deeper with each word and lit up when a thought was finished and he had been able to bring it within the scope of his understanding.

For almost two months Srinigar seemed like an island,

separated from the rest of the world by an icy sea. Days passed and even the buses failed to arrive. The mountains became whiter and their reflection on the frozen, glass-like lake challenged the observer to determine which was reality. All Srinigar seemed topsy-turvy, at the mercy of winter.

Then, for several days the sun shone and the activity of the thaw took over the city. The ice cracked and melted into watery pools, the brown frame houses took on a golden look, the gray of the city became touched with orange and blue and the people began to move a bit more quickly, toward the new work to be done. Little boats loaded with vegetables appeared from nowhere as if by magic. Houseboats were cleaned, scraped and readied for the spring and summer visitors.

Katie took part in the new activity, visiting schools, institutions and homes. She talked with public officials and businessmen, politicians and religious leaders. Her enthusiasm each evening was contagious and, no matter how seemingly mundane, each experience held some new wonder for her.

These were also days for hikes into the mosque-topped hills surrounding the valley. The mosques were always cold and vacant, with large carpeted rooms, fantastically carved walls of stone and hardly a window through which the now warm sun could shine. There were more boat trips on the lakes and canals and walks through the bazaars.

One evening Habib informed us that the plane from Delhi would probably be able to come in the next day. I had already stayed in Srinigar much longer than planned and, since the possibility of another freeze was imminent and a ticket could be arranged, I made plans to leave at once.

That night we had an unusually elaborate feast and invited several of the friends we had made, during our weeks in the valley, to be our guests. It was a clear and beautiful night. The moon was white, lighting Srinigar with a soft white-black winter glow.

The party was a noisy, happy one. Mr. Atal and several of the other guests made advances to Katie which she smoothly rebuffed, smiling at me with bright eyes and a wink. Left to themselves the men embraced happily, danced together and kissed each other joyfully. It was late when the festivities ended. Goodbyes were flowery and affectionate, with embraces, kisses and speeches about love, fellowship among nations and the inevitability of future meetings.

Later, when we were alone, Katie told me, "I'm leaving the boat, too. The price is going up and Habib needs it for some of the passengers from the plane. It's better that way. What would I do on this Queen Mary alone? I'm going to that little hostel near the museum. Do you remember it? It has a great view of the canal. There are still so many things I want to do and understand here, but it will be strange without you."

The following morning Katie walked with me to the airline bus station. The cold room was full of people, anxious to be on the first plane leaving for Delhi in several weeks. Habib, always the businessman, was planning his strategy to capture some of the incoming tourists for his boats.

When the airline was announced, Katie hastily left me with a promise, "I'll write on your birthday."

As the bus pulled out onto the slushy road, I looked back. Katie was walking toward the hills, away from the lake. She had left her blanket on the boat that morning and was dressed as I had seen her the first day in her baggy, black angora sweater, too tight ski pants and Indian sandals, splashing in the slush as she walked.

We left Srinigar on schedule, rising slowly above the

valley with the plane's two motors straining for height and speed. Below, the streets seemed empty; the boats along the river, scattered among the lake islands, looked like colored squares on a black-brown rug.

When we passed the hill of the mosque, it seemed to me I could see a black-clothed figure of a girl seated on the steps. Her arms were encircling her legs which were pulled up under her chin. Her head was raised, face upward. For an instant we seemed to feel each other's vibrations. She remained motionless as the plane turned to bank between two towering mountains and veer off into the clouds.

chapter 12

Nepal

We need not climb the mountain to see into the valley. All things to be seen can be found in a simple shared bowl of rice.

Lato

"What I really came here for was to hear a crystal-clear temple bell ring across the Himalayas in the early dawn," I told him jokingly. Mohan looked very serious. "Why should you not hear such a bell?" he asked.

I had been in Katmandu for only a week and had met Mohan at the small hotel annex where I was staying. He was hotel manager, tour leader, kitchen boss, host and general do-all. He was twenty years old, a very handsome, extremely dark-skinned Indian who had become weary of his country and emigrated to Nepal. His family lived in Delhi, and he had been living alone for several years in this new country which he loved.

The annex he managed was a part of a more expensive, more centrally located hotel. It had only four rooms, to accommodate any overflow from the main hotel, one bath and a small dining room. There were only two others staying at the annex, a rather jolly, retired German gentleman and his wife, both very young looking, brimming with energy, activity and life. After a few hours we had all become fast friends and formed a close-knit family with a home of our own.

On the afternoon I expressed a desire to hear the temple bell, we were resting in the hotel garden which faced the giant Himalayas. The sun was warm. It was the month of March, spring.

"I have a good friend who was born in this valley. He would know where we could go to hear your bell," Mohan told me. "Shall we visit him tonight? He is a student and it is now vacation time so it is well to go at once."

"Ja! You must go at once!" the German woman echoed in a throaty tone. "We are not young enough to go along, but you must experience dawn in the Himalayas. We already know the valley floor. There is not a street we have not walked through in Patan or within twenty miles. So why not go?"

That evening we visited Tara in his rooms off the main street in the center of Katmandu. He was a small boy, not over sixteen years of age, with a rather round, almond-eyed face which made him look even younger. He had a winning smile and fine even teeth. As he was studying English in school, he was pleased to have someone with whom he could practice. He was delighted by our visit.

"Yes, I can go at once," he said. "When shall we start?"

It was as simple as that. We made our plans for the end of the week, just a few days off.

"I know many beautiful villages," Tara told us. "We shall follow the river through the great valley, then go up into the mountains to the tiny village of the bells."

Our German friends hired a jeep, and on the morning of our departure, drove us to the end of the road. Here a narrow, well-worn path began which led up a slight incline before abruptly plunging down into the spectacular valley of Nepal.

It was dawn and in the distance, washed orange and blue, stood Annapurna, Everest and others of the world's most lofty and beautiful mountains.

Tara had instructed us to bring only a wool blanket and the clothes we had on and Mohan had packed a lunch to tide us over until we reached the first village late that afternoon.

We said goodbye to our friends and started our descent into the valley. In the distance we could see a silver snake of river winding along and finally vanishing into the mountains.

"We follow that river," Tara said.

For the next several miles we chatted gaily, sang in English and Nepalese, and spoke of our dreams.

Mohan was content to stay in Nepal forever. He had met a girl, eleven, who was now going to school but would soon be ready to marry. The hotel would be their home. They would always have food and warmth. They would have many children.

Tara, on the other hand, wanted to see the world. He was eager to see great India. The United States was far too remote for his young dreams, but of course he would some day like to go there. He would never marry.

At mid-day we stopped and had our lunch of Indian chapate and curried vegetables with cold rice, and drank from the icy mountain streams which seemed to follow the path into the valley. The sun was warm and the valley below appeared totally uninhabited.

When we reached the river it was late afternoon. The sun still was hot, our bodies were warm and the single wool blanket we each carried had taken on gigantic proportions. We were delighted to stop at the river's edge, drop our blankets, strip and bathe in the icy stream. Mohan produced a bar of soap and we all scrubbed ourselves free of dust and dirt. Tara washed his clothes, too, then we all lay naked in the sun. The only sounds were those of a small waterfall that dropped its meager burden into the river's flow, and of the river itself which rushed through the valley at great speed, as if it had some place to go, some rendezvous to keep.

Tara asked me to sing a song he loved, one I had sung casually for him a few days earlier, and often since, at his request.

"Summertime, when the living is easy..."

He listened intently and finally said, "I must learn that song. I like it much."

We reached the first village at nightfall. It was a simple cluster of wooden structures, each two stories high with narrow ladders up to large communal rooms. The lower stories were divided, with one open room and the other closed for eating and sleeping.

Our arrival caused a crowd to gather, which looked like the entire village population. Very animatedly, Tara talked with them. It soon became clear that Tara was explaining our presence, telling them who I was and that I came from a far-off land, the United States. He also explained, he told me later, about the crystal-clear bell. No one questioned this motivation, rather they offered suggestions as to where the best bell could be found. They smiled warmly, welcoming us.

A place for us to sleep was arranged on the upper level of one of the houses. One side of the room was open to the night. A candle was brought and then food was carried to us on a large wooden tray. It was rice and dahl, a mixture I was to eat frequently during my stay in the valley. The dahl, though it varied in appearance and consistency, most often seemed like glue and tasted like chives and exotic spices. I was shown how to mix the rice and dahl with my fingers and feed myself by the finger load. It was warm, rather good and always filling.

Tara chattered freely with the group which gathered to watch us eat. He asked them to sing. Their songs sounded tunefully romantic, without the dissonance of Indian music—romantic yet not Western. They sounded rather sad. It did not surprise me then that they were delighted with "Summertime" which they insisted I sing for several encores.

As soon as the sun was out of sight, the night turned icy cold. We finished our dinner in the candlelight, washed it down with hot tea and then Tara announced it was time for us to sleep. He explained that we had a long, difficult journey the next day. The group dispersed. Mohan spread one of the blankets over some straw, placed me in the center with Tara and himself at either side, then pulled the remaining two blankets over us. We were happy, excited, exhausted, and sleep came easily.

There was much activity when we awoke the following morning. Small fires were burning with streaks of smoke rising to the cold, gray, still sunless sky. Everyone seemed to be busily moving about but I was uncertain as to why or to where.

We rose and Tara led us directly to the river for the ritual of the daily toilet; washing our hands, face, chest and brushing our teeth in the icy water.

When we returned to the house, chapates were waiting for us, filled with a tasty, firm cream, and followed by very hot tea. There was also a strong goat cheese.

By the time we finished our breakfast, it seemed as though the entire village population had disappeared. The huts and shacks were empty except for a few very old men and women who sat huddled about the fires and several small children whose flat, slanty-eyed faces seemed to be forever enlivened by smiles. I cannot remember ever hearing one of them cry.

We gathered the blankets and resumed our trip across the valley floor. We stopped only for lunch which we had purchased in the morning and for a short swim and rest in the afternoon. Tara seemed pulled in an unknown direction, seemingly into nowhere, but there was never any doubt that he knew exactly where he was going. Our goal that evening was to reach the end of the valley and start the ascent of the tall mountain which already blotted out most of the sky before us.

The paths were deserted, except for occasional groups of Nepalese with giant loads on their backs, going or coming, from nowhere, it seemed, to nowhere. We also passed several Tibetans, colorfully garbed, with masses of jewelry and tattooed faces.

At dusk, we reached our destination, simply a dozen stone houses. Somehow, villages seemed to appear from nowhere just when we felt we were too tired to go on.

As before, people came out to meet us and ask the usual questions. Fires, to which we were welcomed, were soon lit and the smell of food filled the night air. Lodging was never any problem. Everyone seemed pleased to share what he had, though it was clear that there was neither much spare room nor any excess of food.

Our host that evening was a small man and, like most of the Nepalese I had seen, it was impossible to guess his age. His frame was solid and his muscles strong. His eyes were narrow and bright, his face round, and his head was topped by a pointed hat which made him look like a bright pixie. His name was Lato.

As we walked toward his house he questioned Tara about

me, stealing quick glances in my direction, smiling, and shaking his head in what appeared to be a gesture of approval, which he repeated many times.

The house was simple, again with two levels. We were taken upstairs where there were two sleeping rooms, both quite small and windowless. There was no furniture in the house. A hole for a fire and some large iron utensils were the only frills.

We laid our blankets on the straw at one end of the room and prepared for darkness when, from necessity, much activity must stop.

Lato was married and had two small children. His wife was not over sixteen years old, thin, and extremely shy, with a pretty young face. She moved about the house quickly, with few lost motions and the agility of a small squirrel. Lato told us that she would fix chicken and we would have a real feast; she would also fix fresh chapate, dahl and get milk from the cow.

In less than an hour everything was ready, and she shyly placed the food before us. Lato had seated himself next to me and continued cementing our friendship with glances of warmth and gentle smiles. He praised his wife and pointed out the high quality of her cooking. From time to time he questioned Tara.

"How far was this United States, in days, from Katmandu; on foot, of course?"

"What was life like there?"

"Did they eat such good dahl?"

Lato was a person for whom words were superfluous. His every look communicated far beyond the limit of spoken language.

"Take more food, please. I am concerned that you have not eaten enough," Tara translated unnecessarily. "I am so pleased that you have chosen my house to honor with your presence. You are welcome to stay forever."

Lato served the dinner, first to me, then to the others and finally to himself, taking what was left. I was becoming very fond of Lato and wanted to know more about him. When he left us for a few minutes, I asked Tara to tell us what he knew about our host.

Like all the others in the valley, Lato was a farmer. He was wealthier than the others and had several animals, among them a cow, two pigs and several chickens. His house was in a most advantageous position, quite near the water pump. He had been born in the valley and had traveled as far as Katmandu only once in his life. Neither his wife nor his children had ever been so far. All of his children attended school for a portion of the day, the rest of the time he taught them the skills necessary to maintain his position as one of the valley's best farmers. He was highly respected in the village, not only for his skill as a farmer and his strong back, but also for his keen mind. So much was this true that a retired teacher from Katmandu, who had come to live in peace in the valley, had chosen Lato as his best friend and intellectual companion.

When Lato returned, the village was already in total darkness. The moon was almost full and cast a soft white over the dirt streets. The houses, having assumed the night glow, seemed less harsh and ragged.

Lato had brought us two prizes: the teacher who, to my delight, spoke good English, and several bottles of the celebrated Nepalese rum.

In what seemed no time at all, we were feeling the effects of the warm conversation and the potent drink. The teacher was never at a loss for words. He was a Hindu and as the magic of both communication and rum took effect, he shouted freely from Hindu scriptures, addressing no one in particular.

Lato listened intently as if there were an opportunity at this moment to gain some new insight, to learn about some new mystery.

"A man should not hate any living creature. Let him be friendly and compassionate to all. He must free himself from the delusions of 'I' and 'Mine,'" the teacher shouted.

He poured himself more rum, then continued. "Wisdom is the secret of secrets. Knowledge is the holy of holies, the god of gods, and commands the respect of crowned heads; shorn of knowledge, man is but an animal."

The philosopher kissed me squarely on the mouth, "Oh, who has created the two letters mitram (friend), which are more precious than a mine of gems?" He was very drunk by this time.

During this period our host had, in the manner of the Nepalese, cuddled close to me, and with his hand in mine, rested his head on the stone wall behind us. He seemed to breathe in the joy of the scene like a lover.

As more liquor flowed, the group rose and danced. How strange it seemed that, high in Nepal, at the very base of the Himalayas, a group of people, hardly able to communicate, who just yesterday had not even known each other, were now singing and dancing in the night like brothers.

In the midst of the gaiety a voice called from the street below. Tara explained that it was Lato's young wife calling him to come to bed. Lato told her that I was a very special guest, that there would be no sleep that night, that she should go to bed and stop her absurd sniveling. She became silent at once, but from time to time she could be seen below, her tiny figure silhouetted by the bright moonlight, waiting.

One by one, we fell in exhaustion onto our blankets and, huddled in each others' arms, fell asleep. The teacher muttered drunkenly in my ear, "Remember, one should not see the sun at the time of rising...so say the Purnas and so does the Lord require." Having said this, he pulled a corner of the blanket over his head and instantly emitted a large snore.

We awakened late the following morning. Our host was outside waiting for us to rise. At his signal his wife shyly brought breakfast and set it beside us. Except for the teacher, none of us felt much like eating but, not wanting to insult our hostess, we forced the food into our mouths and swallowed it as best we could. I tried to tell her how grateful I was for everything that she had done for us. She seemed to understand and smiled delightfully.

Tara insisted that it would be bad taste to try to pay for their hospitality and taught me to say "thank you" instead. When I accomplished this, Lato's face broke into a broad smile. He embraced me tightly, almost crushing the wind from my body, and kissed me. There were tears in his eyes.

All the village came out to watch our morning toilet. They gazed at me in wonder as the teacher told them about the stranger. Lato supplied us with some hard-boiled eggs, freshly cooked chapate and crisp apples and we were ready to continue our voyage.

"Will you not stay, just for a few days?" Tara translated, but we assured Lato that we were in a great hurry. When we embraced for the last time, it hurt me deeply that I would never see this man again—he, to whom I had been so close, who had shared with us his home, his food, his love, with no hesitation or thought of gain, simply for the pleasure of knowing another human being. This time, we both cried.

The climb to the next village was not an easy one. Indeed, there were moments when I began to wonder if this had not been a rather insane idea. The ascent, like most of those in Nepal, traced the shortest distance between two points, regardless of the steepness of the path or the dangers involved. This time, as we climbed, we could not even find the energy to sing.

From time to time we came upon other travelers, always friendly and willing to stop for a short chat with Tara. If there was a girl in the party, Tara and Mohan would make teasing remarks, to which everyone would respond with childlike glee. Except for a short stop for lunch, we continued climbing for the entire day.

Occasionally Tara would ask, "What comes after 'fish are jumping and the cotton is high'?"

Mohan would answer, "Your daddy's rich and your mother's good looking."

"Oh."

Then we would proceed in silence.

By late afternoon we had reached the mountain peak. It was flat, as if nature had leveled it off for the city to be built with a view which could not be surpassed by any other. The main road wound past several impressive buildings, a three-storied palace, a building which Tara referred to as the city hall and a beautiful, rambling temple at the far side of the city.

Tara had hoped we could stay at the palace, but upon inquiry, found that this was not allowed. Instead, we were directed to a large rest house along the main street. It looked out, without obstruction, over the valley several thousands of feet below, and the mountains which surrounded it.

The proprietor was delighted with his guests and gave us an attic room with no furniture. It had two large windows with heavy shutters which looked out over the cliff edge. A small stairway led down to the remainder of the house. The room was cold and a fire was started at once.

Though it was still early afternoon, it already was so

cold that we were compelled to wrap ourselves in our blankets in order to walk through the village.

We went directly to the temple. It sat precariously at the very edge of a cliff which fell, without obstruction, to the valley floor. The walls were of thick stone. Stairs led us upward to a large, vacant worshipping room with several small adjoining chambers. The usual statues of Shiva, the bull, the dancer, the eunuch and the inevitable lingam were all there. The wooden ceiling was intricately carved with naked men and women in complicated positions of sexual intercourse. Tara laughed at these and explained that they were done hundreds of years ago to shock away the sensitive, virginal goddess of lightning.

In an anteroom of the temple, in an open space in the wall, hung two very large bells.

"Here is where you will hear your temple bells," Tara said. "These are very fine bells and can be heard almost to Katmandu."

We descended a stairway to the temple basement, now serving as a schoolroom and crowded with children from seven to seventeen. The teacher himself was very young, not over seventeen years old. Each child held a different lesson, a book, a scrap of newspaper or a bit of written script. Each read his own material aloud with all the others. Some seemed to know their material from memory and seldom looked at the papers they held, but rather watched us with curious eyes. The room echoed with the loud sing-song chant. The teacher wandered back and forth, seriously, before the group, waving a large stick as if he were conducting a choir.

When we left the schoolroom, the sound of the youthful voices followed us through the village streets, echoing from the small huts which lined the road, down to the water fountain on the hillside.

The water fountain seemed to be the center of activity. Here, half-naked villagers washed their yellow-brown bodies and the women chatted as they filled their water pitchers; several women were laundering clothes, while others just stood about, watching and chatting. Tara and Mohan entered easily into the spirit of things and were soon taking part in the general activity.

"I have asked a few of the villagers to come to our room this evening," Tara told me later. "They were interested in talking with you. They would like to hear about your country and your people."

After our usual rice and dahl dinner, the guests began to arrive. I was introduced to the Mayor's son, the school teacher, the innkeeper and his two sons, and several others whom I had seen at the fountain. They all sat cross-legged before me in silence, waiting for me to speak. It was very difficult to know where to begin or what to say. In trying to find something we seemed to have in common, I decided to start with the family and the home. The group listened carefully to every word, as if they actually understood me, and responded to Tara's translations with audible wonder and gestures which seemed to say "Did you hear that?"

Their questions were simple but revealed that there had been communication. It was apparent that a bridge between our cultures was a difficult one to grasp, so differently did we live, feel, perceive.

Tara had ordered rum which was passed around. The bottles made several journeys through the group and soon we all became a bit noisier, more responsive and affectionate. We began to sing. Instruments were produced and the room became filled with the plaintive music. By the time the dancing began, we had a great deal in common: we were a group of happy human beings.

Morning came much too quickly. An orange sun streaked

into our dark room to announce the dawn. At once, loudly, beautifully, a crystal-clear temple bell rang out through the cold morning air. I jumped to my feet, shouting to Tara and Mohan, then rushed down to the street to follow the sound of the bell. The temple was bright orange, as was the whole village. Shadows of pale purple and faint colors of blue and red made accents of shadow spots.

The bell rang with a measured clearness. It seemed quickly to reach the distant peaks of Annapurna and Everest in the distance and awakened the dawn to fill the valley with morning light.

Tara and Mohan watched the scene with sleepy eyes. We felt great empathy. People are easily united in beauty. No one spoke. We were at one with everything and words were not needed. The bell continued to ring for some time into the unknown and seemingly beyond.

We walked back to the rest house in silence. I had heard my temple bell ringing across the Himalayas in the early dawn.

All at once I was very tired, drained, exhausted. I blamed it on the altitude, the excitement, the rum. I thought of Lato, somewhere in the valley. Did he, too, hear the bell? Was he still wondering about me and my world as I was about him? Could either of us ever truly explain to anyone else what we had experienced that evening together?

I suddenly longed to lie between Tara and Mohan, under our wool blankets, close my eyes and sleep.

Epilogue

Traveling THE WAY OF THE BULL leads nowhere. If one needs to attach a meaning, it lies merely in traveling the WAY creatively—in wonder, in joy, in peace and in love.

This book described a short part of my voyage, some of the teachers I met along the WAY and what they taught me. It is neither a guide nor a map and if you follow my WAY you will surely get lost. It is merely a sharing. For *my* WAY can only be mine, as, someday, if I stay with it, it will lead me back to myself. *Your* WAY can be equally exciting, as it will lead you back to you, the only place where you can ever *become*.

Travel joyously.

Leo F. Buscaglia

About the Author

DR. BUSCAGLIA is also the author of the classic favorite, *Love*. *Personhood* and *Living, Loving and Learning* have both become national best sellers. Dr. Buscaglia devotes his time and energies to helping others share in a better understanding of life and love.